MKM RESEARCH LABS

HANDBOOK OF MODEL RISK MANAGEMENT FOR VENDORS

First Edition: TBD

ISBN: TBD

By David K Kelly
Chief Science Officer
MKM Research Labs

Edited by Johnny Mattimore
Chief Executive Officer
MKM Research Labs

Copyright Statement

ABOUT THE AUTHOR

David K Kelly is a seasoned investment banking professional with 30 years of experience, having held senior leadership positions in the front office and risk departments at global GSIB Banks [1]

His entrepreneurial ventures include his most recent role as co-founder and Chief Science Officer of MKM Research Labs, a research company focused on developing and donating open-source business solutions for finance. This includes developing a market in a new asset class: Physical Risk Swaps.

Throughout his career, David has demonstrated expertise in implementing advanced modelling solutions for capital requirements under new regulatory frameworks. He is a leading advocate for Model Risk Governance for vendors that provide data and analytics to finance; and, in particular, the regulatory demanding governance in the global banking system

David's educational background includes a first-class degree in Mathematics from the University of Bristol in 1989 and Honours in Advanced Studies (Part III) in Pure Mathematics from the University of Cambridge in 1990.

---

[1] GSIBs - with link - https://www.fsb.org/2024/11/2024-list-of-global-systemically-important-banks-g-sibs/

ABOUT THE EDITOR

Johnny Mattimore has over 35 years in financial services. He originally trained as a mathematician and market economist working on major trading floors of capital markets firms. He worked for the first half of his career in investment banking in analysis, trading and structuring.

He then spent the second half of his career in hedge funds and asset management across a range of roles running money, risk management, and trading systems design and integration. More recently, he has focussed his efforts on the integration of cutting-edge risk solutions into the financial ecosystem for banking, insurance and asset management. This includes the development of the new asset class Physical Risk Swaps to manage the substantial and increasing exposure that the financial system (banks, insurers and asset managers) have to asset valuation impact from physical hazard risks.

He is a leading proponent of open-source standards and has a high level of expertise in the integration of data, methods and models into finance for lines of business and group functions. As well as having held mainstream roles in large organisations, he has a long history in developing new businesses, particularly in hedge funds and fintech.

Johnny graduated from the University of Bristol, UK, in 1988 with a BSc in Mathematics. He has written extensive research throughout his career, including major works for risk, emerging markets, structured debt and investment methodologies, ranging from discretionary to systematic.

ACKNOWLEDGMENTS

To my lovely wife, Victoria, and my wonderful children, David Henry, Georgina, and Angus. And, of course, not forgetting Otis!

A Special thank you to Reza Moaleji; for the journey!

TABLE OF CONTENTS

This page is intentionally left blank

FOREWORD

This new publication on Model Risk Governance for Banking is part of the long journey that David Kelly and I have been on to solve the enormous challenge of integrating physical risk into the banking system. The book applies to everything done in banking, capital markets, and onwards up to the full aggregation of risk at a bank holding group level under the rigorous standards of BCBS239, the post-2008 framework from the Basel Committee on Banking Standards for risk.

While it applies to the broad scope of banking risk models, data and workflows, it is particularly relevant to the current challenges for integrating physical risk into the banking system. The reason is that the associated data and models for physical risk are all new for the banking system, but can follow the same banking standards and plumbing, even when the components are historically different to other integration challenges the system has faced.

While we have addressed the full supply chain of physical risk data and models in prior publications, presentations, and event panels, this publication is focused on the unique final step: how that supply chain, or any other data and model stack, is required to satisfy the global banking system's model risk governance.

A Tale of Sovereign Solvency, Banking Solvency and a Lone Analyst.

The use of the word "unique" is often overused. However, in the case of global banking, it is apt. This may be explained by the linkage between countries' sovereign creditworthiness and the solvency of their private sector banks.

At the beginning of my career in the 1980s and 1990s, I spent considerable time specialising in emerging markets debt securities restructuring, rescheduling, trading and new structuring. It all started with the restructuring of bank loans to mostly Latin American countries, which was resolved under the auspices of the Brady Plan, after the then US Treasury Secretary Nicholas Brady.

At that moment in the late 1980s, the entire money centre banking system in the USA and their counterparts in other advanced economy countries were on the brink of insolvency. It was compounded in the USA by the 1980s national savings and loans crisis, adding additional stress to the domestic banking system.

During the negotiations, Brady was flanked by two of the most exposed and systemically important banks, Citibank and JP Morgan. At this time, I was an analyst at Citibank, working in the Mortgage-Backed Securities team in New York. I was taking the opportunity as part of my graduate training programme to learn all that I could about securities from a very bright spark called Andy Sparks, head of mortgage and rate strategies for global capital markets.

One afternoon, a senior member of Citibank's Latin American Sovereign Debt Restructuring team came to the hot-house of mathematicians working on the cutting edge of new structured debt for mortgages. The derivatives carved from pools of mortgages were rare and the environment for analysts was rarefied. He casually announced the following (or words to this effect):

"I'm looking for ambitious, hungry, risk-taking analysts who can help us take all of our defaulted sovereign loans (we've got far too many for our own good) and turn them into tradable bonds. I'm told this is the only pool of analysts who have the skills to do this work. It's a risky job - we'll either be a total failure and need to look for new jobs or hugely successful and make lots of money. Do I have any volunteers?"

One lonely hand went up. I was now the only non-Latino in the Latin-American Debt Trading Team. I spent the next few years back and forth between Europe and the Americas. The best decisions I ever made. By osmosis and long hours, I crammed decades of knowledge and skills into just a few years, being exposed to senior management and negotiations I would never have seen if I had chosen a conventional learning route in banking.

What Did I Learn?

In a nutshell, I learned the following, not exhaustive, but the most relevant to inform the rest of my career in global capital markets and to feed into my understanding of the evolution over the next four decades of model risk governance:

Sovereignty: sovereign nations and their private banking institutions are inextricably entwined. When all is going well, the banks are private; when it isn't, the banks are nationalised—something most of the rest of the world only learned decades later in the global financial crisis of 2008 onwards.

Assumptions: Idiosyncratic assumptions by a few can result in the downfall of all. This was characterised in the 1980s by a few CEOs of major banks that eschewed a new paradigm that countries do not go bankrupt - oops! Well, that was a big mistake.

Controls: most banks had poor, in some instances non-existent, controls over large lines of businesses. Moreover, providing that these businesses were making money in the short-term, there was little attention paid to the long-term implications.

Information: data and models were in the hands of very few people - rare skills in a rarefied environment. This meant that very few people could challenge the information flow or indeed understand it, let alone know if it was being gamed by the model creators.

PnL & Trust: validate your own information. Trust is very fickle. It's available in abundance when the sun shines, but evaporates instantly when a storm comes. In short, I learnt to trust no-one, validate my own information and live and die by my own decisions. Blaming someone else is a dead-end - it will never restore your PnL.

Liquidity & Prices: getting back to a cash position is the most valuable strategy - it crystallises your PnL and, hence, your bonus. The price to get out of a position may be painful to your PnL, but having no ability to exit and watching helplessly as prices whiplash and degrade your PnL is worse. Why? Because it destroys not so much your PnL but your personal credibility, which means you can say goodbye to autonomy, bonus and, possibly, career..

So Why Does This Matter for Model Risk Governance?

There are rarely new paradigms - mostly just old tricks wrapped in new packaging. Therefore, anything newly adopted by the banking system requires such stringent and ongoing scrutiny. An innovation typically goes through three stages of increasing relevance to the bank: de minimis risk (think a few positions); meaningful risk (thinks 100s of positions); material risk (think 1,000 of positions with a highly active, large volume interbank market).

The events in Latin America of the 1980s rippled across the globe, impacting nations far and wide - including Nigeria, Philippines and much of Eastern Europe. The 1990s saw sovereign crises abound - the disintegration of the former Soviet Union, the break up of the former Yugoslavia, currency crises in Malaysia, Brazil, Russia, and so many banking scandals that continued well into the early 2000s. This is just the emerging debt markets - but many other crises, scandals and bubbles have followed similar patterns from the 1980s to the 2020s.

The above coincided with a remarkable lubrication of the flow of money around the world. Money could now move faster than ever before, with the consequence that it could also precipitate an acceleration of crisis events at a pace hitherto unseen. We may be able to compile entertaining historical facts such as when Edward III of England defaulted and bankrupted the Florentine banking giants Bardi and Peruzzi in the 1340s. However, we cannot easily anticipate how money may move instantly to induce the next crisis, or what might be the catalyst for capital flight.

This takes us back to my final learning above - Liquidity and Pricing. In many respects, this is all that matters at the end of the game. Can I get a price for the position that I own so that I can exit that position - with a counterparty who will settle in cash in a timely manner? That's how to get out of risk and achieve finality, holding only cash in your domestic accounting currency.

Without robust model risk governance, we will fall at many hurdles, but this last hurdle is what will bring down the whole system if it fails, and all other hurdles are overcome. Moreover, it only takes one link to fail for the dominoes to stall tumbling.

Why Do We Need Model Risk Governance?

In summary, we don't need model risk governance because we must meet the bureaucratic dictates of mandatory banking regulation.

Instead, we need it to protect us from ourselves — whoever we are within the model supply chain — which, as my prior experiences suggest, ultimately revolves around trust to get to accuracy for prices, liquidity and PnL.

I hope you enjoy the read and the ride as you assess how model risk governance drives all change in the banking systems of today and tomorrow.

Johnny Mattimore
CEO and Co-founder of MKM Research Labs

PROLOGUE

A few years ago, a mid-sized software vendor received an unexpected request from their largest banking client: "We need to see your model governance framework." A journey from regulatory panic to competitive advantage followed—a transformation that turned compliance burden into a business differentiator.

It is a pattern that I see repeated endlessly. Today, I see it in the market of physical hazard risk vendors. And yet, I do not see any vendors satisfying the rigorous standards required for model governance to penetrate the financial system successfully. This is particularly acute in banking, where model governance is perhaps the most demanding of any market segment.

This book chronicles that journey and provides a practical roadmap for vendors whose models feed into banking risk decisions and capital calculations. Unlike academic treatments of model governance, this guide is born from real implementation experience, complete with the mistakes, revelations, and ultimate success from building a proportionate, pragmatic approach to model risk management.

The central thesis is straightforward: vendor model governance should prioritise managing actual model risk over striving for perfect theoretical compliance. Instead of assuming that interacting with a bank's model validation team is merely about responding to an overwhelming number of requests, why not establish a model risk framework that offers a level of assurance for both the vendor and its banking and non-banking clients?

In short, establishing a model governance function ideally under the management of a Model Risk Committee demands a cultural shift that, in my experience, takes some time for software vendors to recognise its value. For those vendors that think model governance is to keep the bank's pesky model validators at bay, then they are missing an opportunity, as the regulation around model risk will continue to be onerous, so the demands will continue to ratchet up.

At its most basic, implementing a model framework with all the recognisable attributes of a bank's model validation team shifts the vendor's output onto the list of good actors, which will lead to fewer demands, particularly when things go wrong (as they will inevitably do) or when models are migrated or updated. As I frequently joke with my model owners, Tumbleweed in the form of no follow-up requests for information, more testing, and documentation is the best outcome.

The hardest cultural change for a vendor is to discuss, agree and publish their model weaknesses, prescribed limitations of use and proposed monitoring to check the buildup of usage and inappropriate use.

The second-hardest cultural change is the allocation of model ownership and responsibility for its overall performance, way beyond testing. Any framework around models needs a group of quantitative professionals who collectively own the vendor's model risk.

Introducing and running a model governance framework centred on risk instead of box-ticking is a journey worth taking. No bank validation team at the outset will expect everything to be in place other than the declaration of model weaknesses. They will happily receive progress updates as those involved build the necessary artefacts and provide evidence of independent challenge.

Whether facing a banking client's first model governance request or seeking to improve an existing framework, this book provides the practical tools, templates, and insights needed to turn regulatory necessity into business opportunity.

At this juncture, we should all consider the following quote:

"ESSENTIALLY, ALL MODELS ARE WRONG, BUT SOME ARE USEFUL."

Which appeared in Box and Draper's 1987 book "Empirical Model-Building and Response Surfaces". Box's central point was that models are simplifications and, by their very nature, cannot capture every detail of the complex systems they attempt to represent. However, their practical value lies in their usefulness for understanding, predicting, or controlling aspects of those systems, despite their imperfections.

As with any risk discipline, model risk does not eliminate the event of failure but reduces the collateral damage by ensuring models are used judiciously.

In summary, the absence of a vendor's robust model governance will consign them to the endless cycle of pushing water uphill to gain long-term success with end users, which likely will never happen. However, the evidence of model governance that seamlessly integrates with that of an end-user client, like a bank, will ensure decades of vendor competitive advantage, and sometimes enough to knock out the competition altogether.

To end on a lighter note and for those of a certain age, I leave you with this picture of Michael Fish, a BBC weather forecaster, who became famously associated with the storm due to a televised forecast on 15 October 1987[2]. During this broadcast, he remarked:

[2] https://news.sky.com/story/michael-fish-got-the-storm-of-1987-wrong-but-modern-supercomputers-may-have-missed-it-too-11076659

"EARLIER ON TODAY, APPARENTLY, A WOMAN RANG THE BBC AND SAID SHE'D HEARD THERE WAS A HURRICANE ON THE WAY. WELL, IF YOU'RE WATCHING, DON'T WORRY, THERE ISN'T!"

This statement, made just hours before the storm struck, became one of the most memorable gaffes in British broadcasting history. Fish did go on to warn of "very windy" conditions in southern England, but did not predict the scale or severity of the impending storm. The storm that followed was far stronger than anticipated, reducing the town of Seven Oaks to One Oak overnight.

Fish also later admitted that the story about a woman calling the BBC was fabricated, inspired by a colleague's mother's concern about travelling to Florida.

GOOD LUCK AND ENJOY THE JOURNEY!

1.

COMPETITIVE ADVANTAGE

The financial technology landscape has fundamentally shifted. Where once vendors could deliver mathematical models and algorithms with minimal oversight documentation, today's banking clients demand comprehensive model governance frameworks that demonstrate ongoing risk management and regulatory compliance.

This shift isn't arbitrary—it's driven by hard-learned lessons from periodic financial crises, especially the 2008 global financial crisis, and subsequent regulatory reforms. Banks now face intense scrutiny over every model influencing risk decisions or capital calculations, including their third-party vendors. The days when a sophisticated algorithm could speak for itself are over, replaced by a world where transparency, validation, and continuous oversight are not just expected but demanded.

Remember, this is not about whether vendor-supplied data is good for something like basic reporting; it is about whether vendor-supplied data can be used for risk decisions that ultimately impact the stability and solvency of individual financial institutions and the wider financial system.

The core issue for banks is not dissimilar to "Caveat Emptor" when dealing with vendors. The regulators' "Buyer Beware" attitude toward banks states that the banks are responsible for the outcome of the failed model output supplied by a third party. A bank cannot shirk from the reality that it is responsible for models even when it does not own them. To stress the point, here is the core takeaway.

THERE IS NO DELEGATION OF ACCOUNTABILITY FOR MODEL FAILURE FOR FINANCIAL INSTITUTIONS.

Hence, I hear vendors complaining about a blizzard of questions. The mistake vendors make is that they believe that once the questions have been answered to the model validator's satisfaction, the issue is closed without any chance of recurring.

I have also felt that intellectual prickliness coming to the fore as they question why all of the questions. The answer is that the model validator is on the hook. They own the model risk, and they have the right to ask as many questions as they feel like until they are comfortable. If the vendor plays smart, the chances of reaching the right comfort level will disappear. Why would a validator take on the personal risk when they feel that the vendors are, at best, holding back on the correct information?

The transformation in the model governance framework has been surprisingly swift, given its dry subject matter and noticeably unforgiving.

It is natural for vendors to flourish with a good product. Those who once thrived on the elegance of their mathematical solutions now face requests for documentation standards they've never encountered, validation frameworks they don't comprehend, and governance committees they have never even imagined needing to establish.

It's a culture clash of "techs" versus "quants", pitting the rapid innovation cycles that define successful technology companies against the methodical, heavily regulated world of banking compliance.

Vendors flourish in agile development settings, focusing on rapid cycles and ongoing enhancement, valuing the capacity to deploy updates swiftly and adapt to evolving market demands.

This agile approach has served vendors well in competitive technology markets where speed and innovation drive success.

However, traditional model governance frameworks were designed for slower-moving, highly regulated banking environments where stability, documentation, and extensive validation take precedence over speed to market. In summary:

WHILE BANKS DEMAND SPEED TO MARKET, THEY WILL NOT ACCEPT IT AT THE EXPENSE OF HEIGHTENED MODEL RISK.

The collision between these worldviews creates genuine operational challenges. Development teams accustomed to releasing code weekly find themselves constrained by governance processes that require extensive documentation before any change can be implemented. Product managers who measure success in user adoption rates suddenly need to consider model risk assessments and regulatory compliance implications.

The metrics that define success in the vendor world often conflict with the risk management principles that govern banking operations. The largest disconnect we will cover in detail is the difference between testing and model validation.

Resource constraints compound these cultural challenges. Vendors typically operate with leaner teams focused on product development and client delivery, not regulatory compliance infrastructure. The quantitative professionals who build the models are often the same people responsible for client implementations, sales support, and product enhancements. Adding model governance responsibilities to already stretched teams creates resource conflicts that can slow innovation and impact client service.

Unlike banks with dedicated model risk teams, compliance departments, and regulatory specialists, vendors must build these capabilities from scratch while maintaining their core business operations. The investment required to establish proper governance frameworks can seem disproportionate for smaller vendors, particularly when the immediate business benefits aren't clear.

However, getting it right is the difference between winning a client tactically for a short-term revenue uptick that then faces huge client model governance issues versus laying the foundation for winning multiple clients strategically for medium and long-term revenue without any material model governance issues. Now, that's a competitive advantage.

Expertise gaps pose another major challenge. Model governance demands specialised knowledge of regulatory requirements, statistical validation techniques, and risk management principles that may not be present within vendor organisations. The skill sets that make someone an excellent quantitative developer do not automatically translate into understanding regulatory validation standards or designing effective risk monitoring frameworks.

Many vendors discover that their brilliant Phd folk in a myriad of endeavours—mathematicians, data scientists, astrophysicists, nuclear scientists, meteorologists, atmospheric physicists—and experienced software engineers need to learn an entirely new language of model risk management, regulatory compliance, and banking operations. This learning curve can be steep and expensive, particularly when the expertise needs to be built while simultaneously serving existing clients and developing new products.

The consequences of inadequate model governance extend beyond compliance issues. Poor model oversight can lead to production failures that damage client relationships, regulatory findings restricting market access, and reputational damage affecting new business development. In extreme cases, vendors may find themselves excluded from entire market segments if their governance capabilities don't meet banking standards.

They won't know they are being excluded; they will feel that sinking feeling of not getting past the model validators.

NOT HAVING THE RELATIONSHIP WITH MODEL VALIDATION IS "COMPETITIVE DISADVANTAGE" AND IS THE MOST PAINFUL FOR VENDORS - PERSISTENT EXCLUSION WITHOUT A PATHWAY TO RESOLVE THEIR PROBLEM.

The bleak news is that the regulatory landscape continues to shift in ways that raise standards for vendor governance. What might be acceptable now may not meet future requirements, and vendors without solid governance foundations constantly try to catch up as standards evolve. As anyone in banking will confirm, the direction of regulation only goes one way - no regulator is paid to discontinue existing regulation.

The interconnected nature of modern banking systems means that model failures can have systemic implications. Due to the daunting aspects of model interoperability, poor vendor data feeding a pricing model will, in turn, produce inaccurate valuations for the trader and finance. The poor pricing model will also underperform under stress conditions used downstream by the capital model, which impacts the bank's balance sheet, leading to regulatory sanctions.

The competitive impact extends beyond individual sales cycles to market positioning and brand recognition. Vendors known for strong governance capabilities invite themselves to participate in strategic initiatives, regulatory working groups, and industry standards development activities that enhance their market position and provide early insights into regulatory developments.

Competitive Differentiation becomes possible when strong governance frameworks distinguish vendors in crowded markets and support premium pricing strategies. Rather than competing solely on technical features or price, vendors with robust governance capabilities can differentiate themselves on risk management and regulatory compliance—areas where banks place increasing value.

Thus, vendors face a fork in the road. One is to pursue differentiation, which creates opportunities for deeper client relationships and more strategic positioning. Banks view vendors with strong governance capabilities as partners rather than suppliers, leading to more collaborative relationships, longer contract terms, and higher switching costs that protect market position.

The other fork is to pursue a business model that does not correctly address model governance, the "Competitive Disadvantage," which will lead to failure in markets such as banking, despite the allusion of "getting into reporting",—which isn't risk management.

Model governance's documentation, testing, and monitoring requirements create systematic approaches to quality management that benefit all clients, not just those requiring formal compliance. Product development becomes more efficient when governed by clear standards, and client implementations become more reliable when supported by comprehensive documentation.

Market Expansion becomes possible as governance capabilities enable entry into new markets and client segments previously inaccessible. Many vendors discover that implementing model governance for banking clients creates valuable capabilities in other regulated industries such as insurance, healthcare, and government services.

Risk Reduction through a proactive risk management model prevents costly failures and protects business reputation. While the initial investment in governance capabilities requires resources and attention, the long-term benefits of reduced operational risk and improved client relationships often exceed these costs. Avoiding appropriate model risk governance will always prove to be a false economy. Crisis after crisis has shown this to be the case. The evidence is there for all to see.

The challenges outlined above might seem overwhelming, but they are entirely achievable provided vendor leadership recognises a fundamental truth: being smart is not enough. The financial technology industry is full of brilliant people with advanced degrees in nuclear physics, mathematics, computational science, and engineering. These intellectual capabilities are necessary but not sufficient for successful model governance implementation.

The first step toward successful model governance is recognition that vendors must fundamentally shift how they think about their model capabilities. Instead of viewing models primarily as intellectual property or competitive advantages, vendors should take the opportunity to understand how model developers and their validators operate within the heavily regulated world of banking.

The banking industry's approach to model governance isn't bureaucratic obstruction—it's systematic risk management developed through challenging experience with model failures and their consequences. Remember, banks are not just into reporting; they are maintaining systemic solvency, regrettably underwritten by the taxpayers!

Vendors who understand this context can engage with banking clients more effectively and build governance frameworks that meet compliance requirements and business objectives.

The transformation from regulatory burden to competitive advantage is entirely achievable for vendors willing to invest in understanding the banking perspective on model risk and implementing proportionate governance frameworks that address real risks rather than simply checking compliance boxes.

The following chapters will provide the practical roadmap for this transformation, showing how vendors can build model governance capabilities that satisfy banking requirements while supporting rather than hindering innovation and growth. The journey requires commitment and cultural change, but the destination—sustainable competitive advantage in the banking market—justifies the effort required to get there.

THE FIRST STEP IS TO EMBRACE THE UNBEARABLE TRUTH THAT TESTING IS NOT THE SAME AS VALIDATING.

2

WHAT IS A MODEL?

I always pause when I have to explain a model, but in reality, it is a critical first step. Everyone has their own opinion, yet it is surprisingly crystal clear from a regulatory perspective.

"A QUANTITATIVE METHOD, SYSTEM, OR APPROACH THAT APPLIES STATISTICAL, ECONOMIC, FINANCIAL, OR MATHEMATICAL THEORIES, TECHNIQUES, AND ASSUMPTIONS TO PROCESS INPUT DATA INTO QUANTITATIVE ESTIMATES." - OCC

At first glance, this definition might seem overly technical, but it captures something fundamental about how modern financial

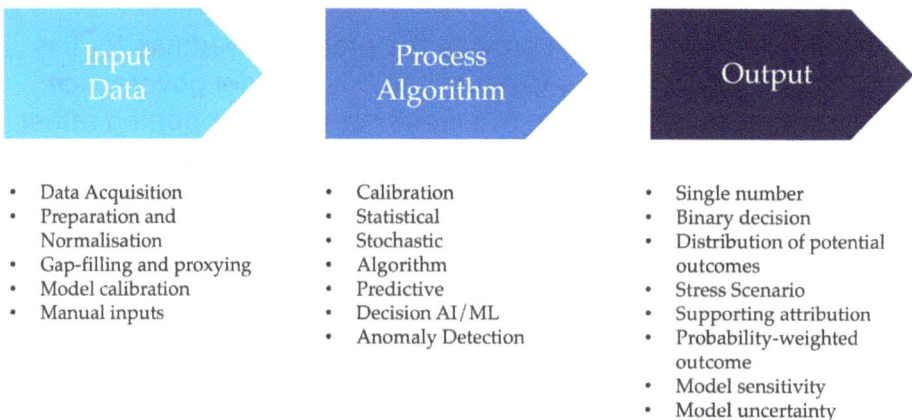

Input Data	Process Algorithm	Output
• Data Acquisition • Preparation and Normalisation • Gap-filling and proxying • Model calibration • Manual inputs	• Calibration • Statistical • Stochastic • Algorithm • Predictive • Decision AI/ML • Anomaly Detection	• Single number • Binary decision • Distribution of potential outcomes • Stress Scenario • Supporting attribution • Probability-weighted outcome • Model sensitivity • Model uncertainty

institutions operate. Banks and other financial organisations rely heavily on quantitative approaches to make decisions about everything from lending money to pricing complex derivatives.

The beauty of this definition lies in its precision; a model must have some intellectual foundation—it can't just be an arbitrary formula someone created. All models, therefore, have in common the same key elements that drive any discussion on model inclusion:-

- Quantitative foundation: Models must use formal techniques from disciplines like statistics, economics, or mathematics.

- Input-processing-output structure: Models systematically transform input data into numerical outputs (estimates, forecasts, or decisions).

- Theoretical basis: Models rely on established theories and explicit assumptions

The input data represents the raw material that feeds the model. This might include customer information, market prices, economic indicators, or historical performance data. But it's not just about collecting numbers.

The input stage often involves significant preparation work: cleaning the data, filling in gaps, normalising different data sources, and incorporating various assumptions about future conditions. Think of this as preparing ingredients before cooking—the quality of what goes in largely determines what comes out.

The processing algorithm is where mathematical, statistical, economic, or financial theories are applied to transform the input data. It might involve complex statistical regressions, Monte Carlo simulations, economic modelling techniques, or financial valuation methods. The key point is that this processing is grounded in established theoretical frameworks that have been tested and validated over time.

The output presents the quantitative estimates used by decision-makers. This could be a single figure (like a credit score), a probability distribution (such as potential losses under various scenarios), or a range of values with associated confidence levels. The output may also include supporting information that helps users understand the reliability and limitations of the estimates.

This structure is so crucial because each component can be a source of model risk. Problems with data quality affect the input stage. Flawed theoretical assumptions or implementation errors impact the processing stage. Misinterpretation or misuse of results creates output-related risks. Understanding this flow helps organisations identify where problems might occur and how to implement appropriate controls.

The transformation aspect is essential. Models don't just organise or display existing information—they generate new insights by applying quantitative techniques to identify patterns, relationships, or predictions that were not obvious in the raw data. This transformation makes models valuable, but it also introduces risks if the underlying assumptions or techniques are flawed.

Understanding what does not qualify as a model is as essential as understanding what does. The regulatory definition helps create clear boundaries, though some situations require careful judgment.

Simple calculations and basic tools typically fall outside the model definition. A spreadsheet that adds up loan balances or calculates simple interest using standard formulas is not applying theoretical frameworks—it's just performing arithmetic. Similarly, basic reporting tools that aggregate and display existing data without any transformation or analysis don't meet the criteria.

Consider the difference between a calculator and a statistical analysis: one merely computes, while the other applies a methodology to generate insights.

PURELY QUALITATIVE APPROACHES ALSO REMAIN OUTSIDE THE MODEL SCOPE.

Expert judgment processes, qualitative risk assessments, and narrative reports may be valuable for decision-making, but don't produce quantitative estimates through formal methodologies.

Standard business applications like general ledger systems, basic accounting software, and transaction processing systems typically aren't models either. These systems perform important functions but execute predetermined rules and calculations rather than applying statistical or economic theories to generate new estimates.

THE KEY DISTINCTION IS WHETHER THE SYSTEM APPLIES ANALYTICAL TECHNIQUES TO CREATE INSIGHTS VERSUS SIMPLY PROCESSING TRANSACTIONS OR ORGANISING EXISTING INFORMATION.

Data management tools represent another category that usually falls outside the model definition. Systems that extract, store, clean, or move data around perform important infrastructure functions but do not typically apply theoretical frameworks to generate quantitative estimates.

However, this boundary can become blurry when data processing involves sophisticated techniques for filling gaps, detecting anomalies, or making inferences about missing information.

Real-world situations often pose challenges in defining what constitutes a model. Complex spreadsheets are a common grey area. While simple Excel calculations are not considered models, more advanced spreadsheet applications that include statistical analysis, financial theory, or economic modelling techniques qualify. The key factors include the complexity of the analysis, the theoretical foundations used, and the importance of the decisions stemming from the output.

Business intelligence and analytics tools present another challenging area. Simple dashboards that display existing data typically don't qualify as models. However, advanced analytics platforms that apply statistical methods, machine learning techniques, or economic models to generate predictions, recommendations, or insights would likely meet the definition. The evolution toward more sophisticated analytics means that tools which once were simple reporting systems may now incorporate model-like functionality.

The practical reality is that technology continues to evolve, and the line between simple tools and sophisticated models can shift over time. What matters isn't the specific technology being used, but whether the approach applies quantitative theories to transform input data into estimates that inform decisions.

THIS SUBSTANCE-OVER-FORM PRINCIPLE ENSURES THAT THE FOCUS REMAINS ON MANAGING THE RISKS THAT ARISE FROM QUANTITATIVE DECISION-MAKING, REGARDLESS OF HOW THAT ANALYSIS IS IMPLEMENTED.

Understanding what constitutes a model has significant implications for organisational operations. When something is classified as a model, it usually becomes subject to formal governance requirements, validation procedures, and continuous monitoring. This isn't merely about regulatory compliance—it acknowledges that models can greatly influence business decisions and results.

The difference between models and non-models helps organisations allocate risk management efforts effectively. A simple spreadsheet that sums basic data doesn't require the same oversight as a sophisticated credit risk model that guides lending decisions involving millions of pounds. Organisations can ensure they address the truly crucial risks by concentrating on systems that genuinely apply quantitative theories to produce estimates.

Start by asking fundamental questions:

- Does the system apply statistical, economic, financial, or mathematical theories?

- Does it transform input data into quantitative estimates? Are those estimates used for decision-making?

If the answers are "yes", you're likely examining a model that requires proper risk management attention. The aim isn't to create a comprehensive list of every calculation within the organisation, but to pinpoint the quantitative methods that could notably influence business outcomes if they fail or are misused. This risk-focused view helps ensure model risk management concentrates on what truly matters for the organisation's success and stability.

As technology evolves and new analytical methods emerge, the fundamental principles behind model definition remain important. Whether used in traditional software, advanced spreadsheets, cloud platforms, or state-of-the-art artificial intelligence systems, the key question remains the same: Does the approach apply quantitative theories to produce estimates that guide decisions? Understanding this difference is crucial for effective model risk management in today's data-driven business world.

The Overall drivers of model risk can be summed up in the following list:-

- Critical output such as risk decision-support and capital.

- High or concentrated usage exploiting a known weakness.

- Inappropriate use outside of its limitations.

- Extensive interoperability and dependency of models.

- Late stage in the development lifecycle.

- Deteriorating performance.

- Unstable model output.

- Lack of output attribution.

- Findings are slow to remediate.
- Drop in the quality of input data.
- Users treat a model as a black box.
- Staff turnover in operations and the end-user group.
- Poor model documentation.

3

TESTING IS NOT VALIDATION

The core point to remember is that the model validator has to own the risk associated with the vendor's model. Testing and documentation are the absolute minimum requirements, but they do not address the risk components that validators need to assess. The vendor should strive to make this risk assessment as straightforward as possible, and that means showing they have gone through a similar thought process that a validator is used to when talking to internal model owners.

Creating the pathway for the validator to walk along increases the level of assurance that the vendor's staff are operating with the right risk mentality and that such mentality is cultural from the leadership team to the coders.

The most common misconception among vendors entering the banking model governance world is the belief that testing equals validation. This fundamental misunderstanding drives much of the frustration and confusion vendors experience when first encountering banking model validation requirements.

TESTING CHECKS THAT THE CODE EXECUTES CORRECTLY ACCORDING TO SPECIFICATIONS AND OPERATES EFFICIENTLY IN PRODUCTION ENVIRONMENTS. MODEL VALIDATION CHALLENGES THE CHOICES MADE BY MODEL OWNERS AND ASSESSES WHETHER THOSE CHOICES ARE APPROPRIATE FOR THE INTENDED USE.

Model validation operates on two distinct levels. First, it validates and challenges the model owner's various choices across several aspects of the model.

Second, validation identifies known model weaknesses and limitations of use. No model is perfect, and validation requires honest assessment of where models might fail or produce misleading results.

This is not a "Gotcha!" exercise - it is not about finding faults to criticise—it's about understanding boundaries of utility so models can be used appropriately.

The implementation stage comes later, when a model combines input data and a calculation engine to create the production system that clients purchase. Implementation validation ensures that the way the model is used in production remains appropriate and that all the declared limitations are correctly observed.

Vendors naturally focus on technical excellence. Their models work correctly, produce consistent results, and handle large datasets efficiently. When banking clients start asking about model assumptions and alternative methodologies, vendors often interpret this as questioning their technical competence.

Validators ask about model weaknesses, deepening the confusion. Vendors wonder why anyone would highlight limitations when the model performs well under normal conditions.

THIS PERSPECTIVE MISSES THE FUNDAMENTAL PURPOSE OF VALIDATION–UNDERSTANDING MODEL RISK SO THE MODEL CAN BE USED SAFELY WITHIN ITS APPROPRIATE BOUNDARIES.

Banking validators do not question technical ability. Highlighting weaknesses ("but my model is perfect!" as one vendor quant scolded me, or "there is no model risk here as it is all user-defined") does not destroy the sales process; in fact, it should improve its safe passage, as transparency is the end goal.

A model validator assesses whether the model owner understands their choices and can articulate why those choices are reasonable for the intended application. This assessment requires an entirely different type of analysis than software testing provides.

Model validation includes an essential challenge that testing cannot provide.

WHERE TESTING ACCEPTS SPECIFICATIONS AS GIVEN, VALIDATION QUESTIONS WHETHER THOSE SPECIFICATIONS MAKE SENSE.

Why this methodology rather than alternatives? Are the underlying assumptions reasonable for the intended use case? How do we know this approach will work under different market conditions?

This challenge isn't adversarial—it's protective. Banking validators need confidence that model owners have thought through their design choices and can defend them under scrutiny. Models that can't withstand this challenge may work perfectly from a technical standpoint, but still pose unacceptable risks when used for banking decisions.

The challenge function requires independence from the development function. Developers naturally want their models to work and may unconsciously discount potential problems. Independent validators bring fresh eyes to model assessment and ask uncomfortable questions that development teams might prefer to avoid.

Many vendors make the grave mistake of submitting user-focused technical documentation to banking validation teams, expecting this to be sufficient. We cover this in more detail when we show the entire model development lifecycle.

User documentation covers the how-to aspects of model implementation—how to install the software, configure parameters, interpret outputs, and troubleshoot common issues. This documentation serves an essential purpose for implementation teams, but addresses none of the risk components that validation teams need to assess.

Model validation documentation serves an entirely different purpose. It explains the model's theoretical foundation, design choices, known limitations, and risk characteristics. This isn't about how to use the model—it's about whether the model should be trusted for the decisions it will inform.

The distinction matters because validation teams must own the risk associated with the vendor's model. User documentation that explains how to operate a system provides no insight into whether that system is appropriate for banking risk decisions. Validators need to understand the reasoning behind model design choices, the assumptions that might prove problematic, and the conditions under which the model might fail to produce reliable results.

Understanding that testing and validation serve different purposes is essential for vendors seeking to engage effectively with banking clients. Testing remains crucial for ensuring models function correctly, but validation requires additional capabilities focused on challenging design choices and assessing model appropriateness.

Vendors who grasp this distinction can build governance frameworks that address the real concerns driving validation requirements rather than simply extending their existing testing capabilities. The goal isn't to replace testing with validation, but to develop both capabilities to serve technical excellence and risk management objectives.

4

THEN SR 11-7 HAPPENED

To understand why banks demand model governance from vendors today, we need to rewind to a time when model risk management was largely informal, inconsistent, and often overlooked entirely. Before 2011, banks certainly used models extensively for credit decisions, market risk calculations, pricing derivatives, and regulatory capital requirements. What they lacked was a systematic framework for managing the risks that these models introduced.

Models were typically owned by the business lines that used them, with validation often conducted by the same teams that developed them. The concept of independent model validation existed in some institutions but was far from universal.

Documentation standards varied wildly, model inventories were incomplete or fragmented, and the idea that models could pose significant risks to financial institutions was universally not accepted. Banks do not like to embrace emerging risks in their portfolio of assets until the regulators tell them that it impacts their capital regime.

This informal approach worked reasonably well during stable market conditions, when models behaved largely as expected and their outputs supported the rush to innovation, where caution was thrown to the wind with ever-increasing ways to accommodate leverage in a risk-compression world.

Then "Snap!". The 2008 financial crisis[3] exposed fundamental weaknesses in how financial institutions understood and managed model risk.

---

[3] https://en.wikipedia.org/wiki/2008_financial_crisis

The 2008 financial crisis provided a brutal education in model risk management. Some of the most sophisticated financial institutions in the world discovered that their models had failed them precisely when accurate risk assessment was most critical. These failures weren't primarily technical—the models often functioned exactly as designed. Instead, they were failures of model risk management.

JP Morgan's "London Whale"[4] incident exemplified these risks. The bank's Chief Investment Officer used a model-based hedging strategy, resulting in losses exceeding £6 billion. The internal risk models initially reported that the risk was manageable, but controllers discovered that the trades were far riskier than the models suggested. The failure wasn't in the mathematics but in the risk management framework surrounding model use.

Long-Term Capital Management (LTCM)[5] provided another stark lesson. The hedge fund employed Nobel prize-winning economists and sophisticated mathematical models for arbitrage investment strategies. Despite this intellectual firepower, LTCM lost $4.6 billion in 1998, requiring a Federal Reserve-coordinated bailout. The models worked correctly under normal conditions but failed to capture the extreme market conditions that ultimately destroyed the fund's access to liquidity.

All derivatives models assume immediate access to infinite liquidity, which is true even if you have Nobel prize-winners as your senior quants. When the fund lost money in the billions, counterparts called their positions, making the situation a bloodbath.

The 2008 subprime mortgage crisis revealed systematic model risk issues across the entire financial system. Credit rating agencies had provided AAA ratings to securities backed by subprime mortgages, with these ratings substantially influenced by computer models. These models failed to adequately capture the risks involved, contributing to one of the leading causes of the 2008 financial crisis.

---

[4] https://en.wikipedia.org/wiki/2012_JPMorgan_Chase_trading_loss

[5] https://en.wikipedia.org/wiki/Long-Term_Capital_Management

Between 2002 and 2007, mortgage underwriting standards had significantly deteriorated, which was often masked by models that failed to reflect the actual risks.

The scale and systemic nature of model-related failures during the crisis prompted regulators to develop comprehensive guidance on model risk management.

THE RESULT WAS SR 11-7, "GUIDANCE ON MODEL RISK MANAGEMENT," ISSUED JOINTLY BY THE FEDERAL RESERVE AND THE OFFICE OF THE COMPTROLLER OF THE CURRENCY IN APRIL 2011.

SR 11-7 represented a fundamental shift in regulatory thinking about models. Rather than focusing primarily on the technical accuracy of individual models, the guidance emphasised the need for comprehensive model risk management frameworks that could identify, assess, and mitigate the risks posed by model use across entire institutions.

The guidance has a rare quality found in regulatory texts because it is both clear and concise. This makes it the default reference for explaining why model risk exists and why it must be managed.

SR11-7 established several key principles that would transform how banks approach model risk. First, it broadly defines model risk, encompassing technical failures, the risk of inappropriate model use, and the limitations inherent in all modelling approaches. Second, it emphasised the importance of effective challenge throughout the model lifecycle, requiring independent validation of model development, implementation, and ongoing performance.

Perhaps most importantly for vendors, SR 11-7 clarified that banks remain responsible for model risk even when they don't own the models themselves. The guidance explicitly addressed the use of vendor models and third-party modelling services, establishing that outsourcing model development or operation does not transfer model risk responsibility away from the institution using the model.

THE WIDESPREAD ADOPTION OF SR 11-7 PRINCIPLES CREATED A COMMON LANGUAGE FOR MODEL RISK MANAGEMENT ACROSS THE GLOBAL BANKING INDUSTRY.

Concepts like "effective challenge," "model validation," and "model risk appetite" became standard terminology, enabling more consistent approaches to model governance across different institutions and jurisdictions.

Over the past decade, regulators have increasingly pressured vendors through their banking relationships to demonstrate familiarity with SR 11-7 principles and to provide documentation and governance frameworks that align with these standards. The opportunities were less immediately obvious but equally important—vendors who could demonstrate strong model governance capabilities gained a competitive edge and could participate more strategically in banking relationships.

SR 11-7 established several core principles that continue to shape banking model governance today:

"MODEL RISK CAN LEAD TO FINANCIAL LOSS, POOR BUSINESS AND STRATEGIC DECISION MAKING, OR DAMAGE TO A BANK'S REPUTATION."

This statement elevated model risk to the same level as other operational risks banks were already accustomed to managing systematically.

The concept of "effective challenge" became central to model governance frameworks. This principle requires that models be subjected to independent review and validation by qualified professionals not involved in model development. The challenge function must be ongoing rather than a one-time activity, recognising that model performance can deteriorate as market conditions change.

The guidance also established the importance of model ownership and accountability. Every model must have a designated owner who is responsible for the model's performance and appropriate use. This ownership extends beyond technical oversight to include business responsibility for the decisions informed by model outputs.

Documentation standards became more rigorous and standardised. SR 11-7 specified that banks must maintain comprehensive documentation covering model development, validation, and ongoing performance monitoring. This documentation must be sufficient to enable independent review and replication of model results.

SR 11-7 was never intended to be a static document. The principles it established continue to evolve as regulators gain experience with model risk management and as new types of models and modelling techniques emerge. Recent developments in artificial intelligence and machine learning have prompted additional guidance on model governance for these new technologies.

The lessons learned from the 2008 crisis and codified in SR 11-7 represent hard-earned wisdom about managing model risk effectively. Vendors who understand this context can engage more effectively with banking clients and build governance frameworks that address the real concerns driving these requirements.

SR 11-7 also defined the model governance framework, which outlines the critical artefacts necessary. The subsequent chapter on the Model Risk Committee will cover these.

5

MODEL VALIDATION

The beauty of SR 11-7 lies not in its bureaucratic complexity but in its practical simplicity. Strip away the regulatory language and formal documentation requirements, and you're left with nine fundamental questions that every model owner should be able to answer.

The model validation exercise involves many steps, as the following diagram outlines.

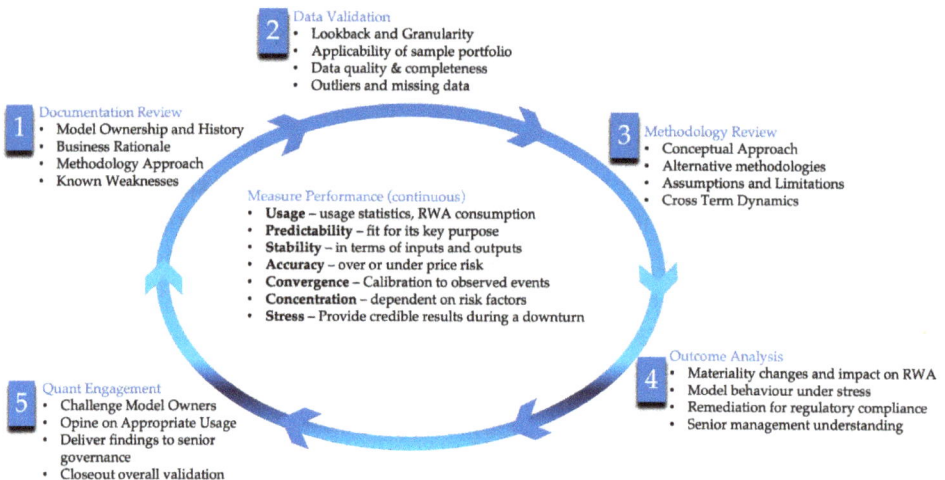

2 Data Validation
- Lookback and Granularity
- Applicability of sample portfolio
- Data quality & completeness
- Outliers and missing data

1 Documentation Review
- Model Ownership and History
- Business Rationale
- Methodology Approach
- Known Weaknesses

3 Methodology Review
- Conceptual Approach
- Alternative methodologies
- Assumptions and Limitations
- Cross Term Dynamics

Measure Performance (continuous)
- **Usage** – usage statistics, RWA consumption
- **Predictability** – fit for its key purpose
- **Stability** – in terms of inputs and outputs
- **Accuracy** – over or under price risk
- **Convergence** – Calibration to observed events
- **Concentration** – dependent on risk factors
- **Stress** – Provide credible results during a downturn

5 Quant Engagement
- Challenge Model Owners
- Opine on Appropriate Usage
- Deliver findings to senior governance
- Closeout overall validation

4 Outcome Analysis
- Materiality changes and impact on RWA
- Model behaviour under stress
- Remediation for regulatory compliance
- Senior management understanding

It is common for vendors to get bogged down in this process, so it makes sense to take a step back and consider what it is a model validation is attempting to achieve (and be seen to achieve)

We can distil what is crucial for model validation by outlining the questions that form the bedrock of model governance and provide a clear framework for vendors to assess and communicate model risk.

These aren't theoretical questions designed by academics—they emerge directly from the painful lessons learned during the 2008 financial crisis and subsequent regulatory investigations. Each question addresses a specific type of model failure that has caused real financial losses and regulatory sanctions. Understanding what drives each question helps vendors provide meaningful responses rather than simply checking compliance boxes.

Question 1: Does the model do what it says on the tin?

This question, sometimes called the "Ronseal test" after the paint company's advertising slogan "It does exactly what it says on the tin", addresses the fundamental issue of model integrity. It asks whether the model implementation is consistent with its theoretical design and intended purpose.

For vendors, this question requires an honest assessment of whether their model documentation truly reflects what the code does. It's not enough that the model functions—it must do so in the manner it claims. Any discrepancies between documentation and implementation introduce model risk, whether those deviations enhance or diminish model performance.

The validator wants evidence that someone has systematically verified that the model behaves as documented across its full range of inputs and operating conditions.

Question 2: Does the model provide timely, accurate and stable results?

This operational question addresses whether users can rely on the model to produce consistent, reasonable outputs under normal operating conditions. It encompasses three distinct but related concerns about model reliability.

Timeliness refers to whether the model can deliver results within the required timeframes for business decisions. A sophisticated pricing model that requires six hours to calculate simple trade valuations fails the timeliness test regardless of its mathematical elegance. Market conditions change rapidly, and models that cannot keep pace with business requirements create operational risk.

Accuracy assesses whether model outputs are correct according to the stated methodology. This does not concern whether the methodology is suitable—that is addressed by other questions—but whether the implementation correctly carries out the chosen approach. Failures in accuracy often arise from coding errors, incorrect data handling, or computational shortcuts that introduce bias.

Stability concerns whether the model produces consistent results when run under similar conditions. Unstable models might produce wildly different outputs for nearly identical inputs, or their results might drift over time without corresponding changes in market conditions. Stability problems often indicate underlying issues with model calibration, numerical methods, or data quality.

Validators want to see evidence of systematic testing across these dimensions, including stress scenarios that push the model beyond normal operating ranges.

Question 3: Does the model consume excessive computational resources?

This practical question addresses whether the computational requirements are reasonable given the model's purpose and the available technology infrastructure. While mathematical sophistication often requires computational power, excessive resource consumption creates operational risk and cost burdens that may outweigh model benefits.

Resource consumption becomes especially critical for models that need to run frequently or in urgent situations. A daily portfolio valuation model that takes 18 hours to complete causes obvious operational challenges. Real-time pricing models that require so much processing power that they impact other system operations present different but equally serious risks.

The question also addresses scalability—whether the model can handle expected growth in data volumes, portfolio sizes, or user demands without becoming prohibitively expensive or operationally unmanageable.

The response to models that consume too much compute time is to scale their parameters down. Dropping a Monte Carlo run from 50,000 to 10,000 iterations, using less granular schemas, or running calibrations less frequently are good examples.

Validators want to understand the trade-offs between computational complexity and practical utility, and whether the vendor has considered alternative approaches that might achieve similar results more efficiently.

Question 4: Are there controls over manual overrides?

This question addresses the governance of human intervention in model processes. Most production models allow users to adjust or override model outputs when they believe the results are inappropriate for specific circumstances. While such overrides can be valuable for handling exceptional situations, they also create opportunities for model misuse and require careful control.

Manual overrides present model risk because they can undermine the systematic approach that models are designed to provide. If overrides become routine rather than exceptional, the actual decision-making process diverges from the validated model, creating undocumented and uncontrolled model risk.

Adequate override controls require clear policies about when overrides are appropriate, approval processes for significant adjustments, and comprehensive override rationale and frequency documentation. The goal isn't to eliminate overrides entirely but to ensure they remain exceptional and are properly governed.

Validators want to see evidence that override capabilities are designed with appropriate controls and that override usage is monitored and reported to relevant governance committees.

Question 5: How is the output consumed for risk decision-making?

This crucial question examines whether users understand how to interpret and apply model results properly in their decision processes. Even perfectly functioning models can create significant risk if end users misunderstand or misapply their outputs.

The question encompasses several related concerns. Do users understand what the model outputs represent and what they don't represent? Are there clear guidelines about how model results should be interpreted in different circumstances? Do users know the model's limitations and how these should affect their decision-making?

Model risk often arises not from failures of the model itself but from misuse by users who do not fully understand what they are working with. Any model supporting binary risk-based decisions, such as a mortgage application, is guilty of presenting recommendations without attaching a probability. Economic forecasts show results like inflation as a single figure, whereas weather forecasts—equally robust—always communicate uncertainty.

Validators want to see evidence of user training, clear documentation of model outputs and their interpretation, and ongoing monitoring to ensure models are being used appropriately in practice.

Question 6: Is the model's output used as input to another model?

This question addresses the "string of pearls" problem—model chains where the output of one model becomes the input to another model. Such arrangements can amplify model risks in ways that aren't immediately obvious and require special attention to ensure overall system reliability.

Model chains create several types of risk. Errors or uncertainties in upstream models can amplify through the entire chain, potentially amplifying rather than offsetting. Dependencies between models may not be obvious to end users, particularly where their underlying assumptions, such as distributions or granularity, are incompatible.

The classic banking example is that to create a VaR calculation for capital, a bank compresses the risk information so that basis risk disappears as all legs are mapped to Risk benchmarks.

The validation challenge becomes more complex because validators must consider whether each model is appropriate and whether the combination of models produces reasonable results. When used together, a well-designed pricing model and a well-designed risk model interact in unexpected ways.

Validators want to see evidence that model interactions have been considered, that appropriate controls exist to monitor model chain performance, and that users understand the dependencies between different model components.

Question 7: Does the model have weaknesses and limitations of use?

The question asks whether the model owner understands and can articulate how the model might fail or produce misleading results.

THIS REQUIRES MOVING BEYOND "OUR MODEL IS GREAT" TO "OUR MODEL IS GREAT FOR THESE SPECIFIC PURPOSES UNDER THESE SPECIFIC CONDITIONS, BUT HERE ARE THE SITUATIONS WHERE IT MIGHT NOT WORK WELL.

Common limitations include specific market conditions under which the model becomes unreliable, data requirements that might not always be met, assumptions that become problematic during stress periods, and computational constraints that might affect model performance under certain circumstances.

The cultural challenge for vendors is that acknowledging limitations feels like undermining the sales process. In reality, transparent discussion of model limitations builds validator confidence because it demonstrates that the vendor understands their model and can be trusted to provide honest assessments.

Question 8: What type of monitoring is required?

Effective monitoring requires understanding what could go wrong with the model and designing specific measures to detect these problems early. For a credit risk model, monitoring includes tracking default rate predictions against actual defaults, monitoring the stability of model coefficients over time, and watching for shifts in the population characteristics that invalidate model assumptions.

The monitoring framework should be proportionate to the model's importance and risk profile. Critical models used for regulatory capital calculations require more intensive monitoring than internal analytical tools. However, all production models need some level of ongoing oversight to ensure they continue to perform as expected.

Validators want to see evidence that the vendor has systematically considered what could go wrong with their model and has designed appropriate monitoring to detect problems before they become serious.

Question 9: Is the overall model risk acceptable?

This ultimate question synthesises all previous assessments to reach a risk-based decision about whether the model should be approved for its intended use. It recognises that perfect models don't exist and that all model usage involves accepting some level of risk in exchange for the benefits that models provide.

The question requires weighing model limitations against model benefits, considering the consequences of model failure against the costs of more conservative approaches, and assessing whether the model's risk profile aligns with its intended use and business importance.

THIS RISK-BASED PERSPECTIVE IS FUNDAMENTALLY DIFFERENT FROM SEEKING PERFECT COMPLIANCE WITH TECHNICAL STANDARDS.

A simple model with well-understood limitations might present lower overall risk than a sophisticated model with poorly understood behaviour. The goal is to make informed risk decisions rather than eliminating risk entirely.

For vendors, this question represents the culmination of the governance process. It demonstrates that they understand their model's risk profile, can engage in informed discussions about risk acceptance with their clients, and so move beyond compliance box-ticking toward genuine risk management.

These nine questions provide a practical framework for vendors to assess their own models and prepare for banking validation processes. They translate abstract regulatory requirements into concrete assessments that guide model development, documentation, and governance activities.

More importantly, they provide a common language for discussions between vendors and banking validation teams. When vendors can demonstrate that they've systematically addressed these questions, validation processes become more efficient and collaborative rather than adversarial.

The questions also scale appropriately to model complexity and business importance. Simple analytical models require simpler responses than complex regulatory capital models, but the same framework applies across the full spectrum of model applications.

The goal isn't perfect answers to all questions—thoughtful, honest responses demonstrate a genuine understanding of model risk and commitment to managing it appropriately.

6

BANK MODEL VALIDATION

The most common question for vendors is whether they should carry out their own independent model validation. The answer is almost always no. Here is why:-

MODEL VALIDATION HAS TO BE PROPORTIONATE TO THE COMPLEXITY AND CRITICALITY OF THE MODEL INVENTORY. THE MOST IMPORTANT ASPECT OF MODEL VALIDATION IS TO SHOW INDEPENDENCE, WHICH CAN BE AS MUCH A MINDSET AS IT CAN BE ORGANISATIONAL.

However, understanding getting the proportionality right requires vendors to appreciate the pain and suffering the bank's model validation team has to endure when validating models. Nobody really likes marking other people's work, but there are reasons why someone who is academically adept to be a front-office quant is in model validation. One is that they see it as a stepping stone to the front office, and others in senior positions have moved out of the front office for a less stressful life.

ONE THING IS THAT MODEL VALIDATORS ARE AS ACADEMICALLY BRIGHT AS THEY ARE HUMAN.

Vendors face fundamental structural challenges, making proper independent model validation that mimics a bank's organisational split nearly impossible.

The independence requirement alone presents a major obstacle—how can a vendor's internal team independently challenge the very models they rely on for revenue? Banks compensate their model validators well, but it's stress/lifestyle-adjusted and so not at superstar levels of the front office. Model validation in the bank's context is a regulatory-imposed charge; it is difficult to find such talent in a vendor that does not contribute to product development and revenue.

The mathematical expertise required for rigorous validation typically exceeds what most vendors can maintain as dedicated resources. These specialists command high salaries and are usually fully occupied with development work, leaving little capacity for the sustained, critical analysis that validation demands.

More problematically, vendor validation teams are typically understaffed relative to the scope of work required. While banks dedicate multiple senior professionals to each validation exercise over several months, vendors often expect a single individual to cover multiple models simultaneously while maintaining regular development responsibilities. This resource constraint inevitably leads to superficial reviews that satisfy compliance checklists but miss the deeper analytical work that constitutes genuine validation.

In short, it is a thankless task whose output falls into the box-ticking mindset. Remember, we are here to run a model risk function with cultural implications.

The independence problem runs deeper than organisational structure. Bank validators can afford to delay or reject models because they aren't responsible for revenue generation from those models. Rejecting a model requires a backbone stronger than wet spaghetti, but a good validator knows they have their organisational position within the Risk department and the regulators on their side.

It's still not easy, but it's achievable when the model is egregiously wrong, and the validator is correct to declare it unfit for purpose. Vendor validators face the impossible task of maintaining objectivity about models that directly impact their company's product development and thus competitive position, with all the financial implications of meeting targets.

However, this doesn't mean vendors should ignore model validation entirely. Understanding what banks actually do during their validation exercises provides crucial insights for vendor governance frameworks and client relationships. More importantly, it demonstrates why the proportionality principle is essential—vendors need governance approaches that acknowledge validation principles without attempting to replicate bank-level processes they cannot effectively implement. Who knows, understanding their challenges might help with dealing with them on a quant-on-quant basis.

T his typical validation exercise would take a mid-ranking validator twelve weeks to complete. More involved models can naturally take much longer.

Phase 1: Planning and Preparation (2-4 weeks)

The validation journey begins with extensive preparation that establishes the analytical framework for everything that follows. This phase often surprises vendors with its complexity because what appears to be an administrative setup involves sophisticated risk assessment and resource allocation decisions.

Validation teams start by developing a comprehensive understanding of the model's role within the bank's operations. This goes far beyond reading technical documentation to include understanding how the model fits into broader business processes, which decisions depend on its outputs, and what would happen if the model failed or produced erroneous results. This business context shapes every subsequent validation decision.

- Collecting and reviewing all relevant model documentation.
- Requesting information from model development teams.
- Confirming validation testing and documentation standards.
- Establishing resource demand and delivery timelines.
- Scope Definition.
- Agreeing on the Quality Assurance framework.

- Confirming regulatory remediation timeframes.
- Agree on the validation approach based on materiality and complexity.

Phase 2: Discovery and Documentation Review (3-6 weeks)

The discovery phase reveals whether the model development process has created the foundation necessary for successful validation. The validator approaches this phase with systematic scepticism, recognising that comprehensive documentation and clear development records often distinguish well-governed models from those that will require extensive remediation.

Documentation review goes far beyond checking that required documents exist. Validators assess whether the documentation actually explains model behaviour, whether development decisions are justified and traceable, and whether the model development team has demonstrated awareness of limitations and potential failure modes. Poor documentation often signals broader governance weaknesses that require deeper investigation.

- Model ownership and development history.
- Material updates in the model code.
- Migration history and implementation tests.
- Business rationale and methodology approach.
- Known weaknesses and limitations.
- Regulatory compliance documentation.
- Gap Analysis of risk not captured in the model.
- Products in live production that use the model.
- Existing documentation to highlight gaps.
- Current internal model validation findings.
- Outstanding audit points.

Phase 3: Technical Validation (6-12 weeks)

The technical validation phase represents the analytical heart of the validation exercise, where mathematical rigour meets practical risk management. The level of analytical sophistication must match the complexity of the validated models—a principle that drives both the depth of investigation and the expertise required.

Like airline crash investigators who must understand aircraft physics at a deeper level than pilots or engineers, model validators are subject matter experts who bring specialised analytical perspectives that often exceed the technical depth of the original model developers.

The Challenge for models built on SAS platforms or incorporating artificial intelligence presents particular validation challenges that can dramatically increase both time and cost requirements. SAS-based models often contain decades of accumulated logic, macros, and data transformations that require line-by-line examination to understand fully. Every data step, procedure call, and conditional statement must be traced to ensure the implementation matches the intended methodology.

AI and machine learning models present even greater challenges because their decision logic may not be directly interpretable. Validators must understand the mathematical algorithms underlying model predictions and how training data, feature selection, and model tuning decisions affect outputs. This often requires building alternative models using different approaches to verify that the AI model's behaviour is consistent with theoretical expectations. We have a chapter dedicated to AI later in the book.

One of the most resource-intensive validation approaches involves constructing independent verification models replicating the original model's functionality using different methods or platforms. These alternative models prioritise mathematical accuracy over computational efficiency, focusing on capturing all risk elements and model configurations correctly rather than optimising for production performance.

At this point, best practice in the model development cycle is to build a model to build its core functionality in some isolation. Usually, the model developer can complete the Ronseal test in Excel or Python. The model can be replicated in an environment closer to production and a more appropriate language. The initial model instance becomes part of the testing suite, so the model that finds its way into production always has a reference twin to check that accuracy has not been lost in the migration.

The alternative model approach serves multiple validation purposes. It provides independent verification of model outputs across different scenarios, reveals whether the original model's mathematical approach is the only reasonable method for the given problem, and exposes potential weaknesses or limitations that might not be apparent from examining the original model alone.

However, building alternative models only works when they are general calculating behemoths, such as a Monte-Carlo simulator, that can be refactored for different model validations.

Model validation requires testing model performance across scenario ranges that far exceed normal business conditions. Validators deliberately attempt to break models by feeding them extreme inputs, unrealistic parameter combinations, and stress conditions that push them beyond their intended operating ranges. This extreme testing reveals whether models fail gracefully or produce dangerous outputs when stressed.

The scenario testing process involves exploration of the entire input parameter space, not just the ranges typically encountered in business operations. Boundary condition testing examines model behaviour at parameter limits and transition points where mathematical algorithms might behave unexpectedly.

Edge case testing explores unusual combinations of inputs that rarely occur in practice but could appear during market stress or operational disruptions.

Stress scenario testing targets conditions that could expose model weaknesses during adverse market conditions. These scenarios often combine multiple stress factors simultaneously to test whether models can provide reliable guidance when banks most need an accurate risk assessment. The goal is to ensure that models support sound business decisions even when market conditions challenge their underlying assumptions. Here is a sample of typical testing over the data usage, methodology and performance:-

- Data Lookback and granularity testing.
- Applicability of sample portfolios.
- Data quality and completeness assessment.
- Outlier and missing data analysis.
- Manual overrides.
- Operational instances.
- Conceptual approach evaluation.
- Alternative methodology consideration.
- Assumptions and limitations assessment.
- Cross-term dynamics analysis.
- Usage statistics and risk-weighted asset consumption.
- Predictability assessment for key purposes.
- Stability analysis of inputs and outputs.
- Accuracy evaluation (over- or under-pricing risk).
- Convergence and calibration to observed events.
- Concentration dependency on risk factors.
- Stress testing to provide credible results during downturns.

Phase 4: Engage Model Developers and Challenge (2-4 weeks)

The challenge phase represents the validation process at its most intellectually demanding, where validators must engage model developers and business users in substantive technical discussions that test the robustness of modelling decisions.

This phase distinguishes professional validation from superficial technical review because it requires validators to challenge fundamental assumptions and methodology choices rather than simply verifying that models execute correctly. This is commonly described as a quant-on-quant discussion that has its own unique pitfalls.

A MODEL DEVELOPER ONCE COMPLAINED THAT A MODEL VALIDATOR ASKED TOO MANY QUESTIONS. WHEN IT WAS POINTED OUT THAT THE VALIDATOR OUTRANKED HIM, HIS RESPONSE WAS TO REMIND EVERYONE THAT THE VALIDATOR WAS ONLY A NUCLEAR PHYSICIST, WHEREAS HE WAS THEORETICAL.

I share this interaction partly because it is as absurd as it is partly true, but also because it shows that within the quant world, where they sit on the hierarchy of academia, it counts. Quant-on-quant interaction between vendors and banks is equally fraught, as academic hierarchy-infested egos get in the way of an objective interaction.

COMPLAINING THAT THE BANK'S MODEL VALIDATOR "DOES NOT GET IT" IS AS IDIOTIC AS IT IS UNCOMMERCIAL. AS THE QUOTE FROM THE FILM LAYER CAKE SUCCINCTLY PUTS IT, "ONLY STUPID PEOPLE THINK THE POLICE ARE STUPID."

Effective challenge requires validators to develop independent perspectives on modelling problems and to engage constructively with model development teams about alternative approaches. This intellectual sparring process often reveals unstated assumptions, identifies potential improvements, and ensures that modelling decisions can withstand scrutiny from qualified professionals who understand mathematical techniques and the business applications.

The senior model validator then needs to:-

- Finalise conclusive validation findings.
- Agree on model weaknesses and limitations of use.
- Agree on remediation timeframe.
- Agree on the overall model risk rating.
- Deliver findings to senior governance bodies.
- Facilitate the closeout of overall validation findings.

Phase 5: Documentation and Sign-off (2-3 weeks)

The final phase transforms months of analytical work into formal documentation that supports ongoing model governance and regulatory compliance. This documentation serves multiple audiences —from technical specialists who need detailed analytical results to senior management who require executive summaries of model strengths and limitations.

The documentation process serves as a quality control mechanism, forcing validation teams to synthesise their findings into coherent recommendations and ensuring that validation conclusions can withstand external scrutiny. The formal sign-off process typically involves multiple levels of review, reflecting the significant business and regulatory implications of validation conclusions.

Final Documentation

- Prepare model validation documentation for handover.
- Ensure submission to model risk governance for approval.
- Plan for the next validation cycle.
- Agree on the following cycle confirmation plans.
- Update status in model inventory systems.

- Establishing ongoing monitoring requirements

The comprehensive testing regimens that professional validation demands require substantial computational infrastructure and time. Testing models across thousands of scenarios, including extreme conditions designed to break model logic, requires dedicated computing resources and sophisticated test management systems, representing significant ongoing infrastructure investments.

Vendors who demonstrate a sophisticated understanding of bank validation processes gain immediate credibility with banking clients. This understanding enables more productive conversations about model risk management, more realistic project timelines that account for validation requirements, and strategic positioning as partners who appreciate the regulatory and risk management challenges banks face.

The ability to anticipate validation questions and provide supporting documentation proactively distinguishes sophisticated vendors from those approaching bank relationships with inadequate preparation. Banks quickly recognise vendors who understand their governance requirements and are more likely to engage in strategic partnerships with vendors who demonstrate this sophistication.

This understanding becomes the foundation for all subsequent vendor governance decisions, providing the context necessary to implement proportionate model risk management frameworks that satisfy both vendor operational requirements and banking client expectations. The goal is not to become a bank but a vendor that banks can trust with their model risk management challenges.

7

MODEL RISK MANAGEMENT

Having established that testing is not validation, we now face an equally important distinction that confuses vendors and banking professionals alike:

MODEL RISK MANAGEMENT IS NOT MODEL VALIDATION.

There I said it! This misunderstanding creates operational confusion, misallocated resources, and missed opportunities for meaningful risk control.

The confusion is understandable. Both disciplines emerged from the same regulatory drivers, use similar terminology, and involve many of the same people. Banking clients often use the terms interchangeably when speaking to vendors, implying that model validation is synonymous with model risk management. This linguistic carelessness masks a fundamental difference in scope, responsibility, and strategic importance.

Model validation is a set of analytical activities designed to assess whether individual models work as intended. Validators challenge model design choices, test mathematical implementations and evaluate performance against stated objectives. Validation operates at the model level, focusing on technical adequacy and appropriate application within defined boundaries.

Model risk management operates at the enterprise level. It encompasses validation as one component within a broader framework for identifying, assessing, and controlling model-related risks across the organisation. Where validation asks whether a specific model works correctly, model risk management asks whether the organisation's overall approach to using models creates acceptable risk levels.

This distinction matters enormously for vendors because banking clients increasingly expect evidence of enterprise-level model risk management, not just individual model validation.

BANKS WANT ASSURANCE THAT VENDORS UNDERSTAND THE CUMULATIVE EFFECT OF THEIR MODELS ON CLIENT OPERATIONS AND CAN MANAGE THE STRATEGIC RISKS THAT ARISE FROM WIDESPREAD MODEL DEPLOYMENT.

This enterprise perspective of model risk management forces consideration of risks that validation cannot address. Model concentration risk emerges when multiple business lines rely on similar modelling approaches, creating vulnerabilities to common failure modes.

Model interconnection risk arises when models depend on each other in ways that amplify rather than offset individual model errors. These systemic risks only become visible from an enterprise-wide perspective.

Model risk management involves strategic decisions that aggregate the technical scope of validation.

- Should the organisation invest in developing proprietary models or rely on vendor solutions?

- How should model risk be balanced against operational efficiency and competitive advantage?

- What level of model complexity is appropriate given the organisation's validation capabilities and risk tolerance?

- At what point will model failure have a material impact on the enterprise?

- Has the stack of models passed its best, and should the enterprise migrate onto a new paradigm?

- What is the key person's risk to those who build and maintain models?

These strategic questions require input from validation activities but cannot be answered through validation alone. The organisation's model risk appetite must consider factors like regulatory capital implications, reputational risks, and competitive positioning that validation teams are not positioned to assess.

The relationship between model validation and model risk management is complementary, not competitive. Effective model risk management depends on robust validation capabilities to provide the technical assessments needed for risk-based decisions. Conversely, validation activities become more focused and efficient when guided by enterprise-level risk priorities.

This integration is imperative, which means that demonstrating validation capabilities is necessary but insufficient for vendors. Banking clients increasingly expect vendors to understand how individual model validation fits within broader model risk management frameworks. They want vendors who can discuss model risk in enterprise terms rather than purely technical terms.

The journey from validation to model risk management requires vendors to think beyond the technical excellence that got them into the banking market.

UNDERSTANDING BANKING CLIENTS AS ENTERPRISES MANAGING COMPLEX PORTFOLIOS OF INTERCONNECTED RISKS RATHER THAN SIMPLY AS PURCHASERS OF MATHEMATICAL SERVICES.

Core to Model Risk Management is the concept of Proportionality, which deserves its own chapter.

8

PROPORTIONALITY

"ALL MODELS ARE CREATED EQUALLY, AND YET SOME MODELS ARE CREATED MORE EQUALLY THAN OTHERS", AN ODE TO GEORGE ORWELL.

The proportionality principle recognises a fundamental truth that vendors often struggle to accept: not all models pose equal risk. A simple linear regression for portfolio reporting requires different oversight than a complex simulator used for capital calculations.

THIS ISN'T ABOUT MATHEMATICAL SOPHISTICATION OR INTELLECTUAL ELEGANCE–IT'S ABOUT BUSINESS IMPACT AND THE CONSEQUENCES OF MAKING MISTAKES.

Many vendors err by applying uniform governance standards across their entire model portfolio. This often leads to one of two issues: either over-engineering governance for simple models, which wastes resources and slows development, or under-investing in oversight for complex, high-risk models, posing unacceptable business and regulatory risks.

Proportionality requires risk-centric assessment of each model across two critical dimensions: materiality and complexity. Materiality measures the potential business impact if the model produces incorrect results. Complexity measures the mathematical sophistication and validation difficulty. Together, these dimensions create a clear framework for determining appropriate governance levels.

I am going to start with the complexity vs Materiality Risk Tier table. The rest of the chapter explains how it works.

Complexity/Materiality	High	Medium	Low
High	Tier 1	Tier 1	Tier 2
Medium	Tier 2	Tier 2	Tier 3
Low	Tier 3	Tier 3	Tier 3
De Minimis	Tier 4	Tier 4	Tier 4

Materiality assessment starts with an honest evaluation of what happens if the model fails.

- **High materiality** models are essential for calculating the firm's performance or client capital. Failure in these models can significantly impact decision-making, and issues might attract regulatory scrutiny.

- **Medium materiality** models cover a moderate percentage of key risk factors. They are important but not critical to core business functions. If they fail, they impact decision-making, but compensating controls exist. Potential regulatory interest may arise in case of problems, but the consequences are manageable.

- **Low materiality** models cover a small percentage of key risk factors with limited impact on critical business decisions. Multiple alternative approaches are typically available, and minimal regulatory concern exists. Failure would have minimal business impact with no direct regulatory implications.

Complexity assessment measures mathematical sophistication and validation requirements.

- **High-complexity** models perform complicated mathematical or statistical operations and incorporate multiple assumptions to which their outputs are highly sensitive. They require specialised expertise for validation and often have significant computational requirements with limited theoretical validation approaches.

- **Medium-complexity** models perform relatively advanced mathematical or statistical operations with some embedded equations and sensitive assumptions. Standard validation approaches are available, requiring moderate expertise for validation and reasonable computational requirements.

- **Low complexity** models incorporate basic analytical operations with few assumptions and slight output sensitivity. Straightforward validation approaches exist, generalist analysts can validate them, and minimal computational requirements apply.

Combining materiality and complexity assessments creates a clear four-tier structure.

Tier 1: Maximum Oversight

Tier 1 models demand comprehensive governance frameworks because their failure could have severe business consequences. These models typically require comprehensive independent validation using multiple approaches, extensive development and validation documentation, continuous performance monitoring with automated alerts, and annual recertification with quarterly reviews.

A practical example of a Tier 1 model is a Monte Carlo simulation that banking clients use for regulatory capital calculations. This model is highly material because it directly affects capital requirements and is highly complex due to sophisticated statistical methods with multiple correlated assumptions.

The governance requirements reflect this risk profile: comprehensive independent validation by qualified quantitative analysts, extensive documentation including theoretical background and implementation details, continuous monitoring of model performance against benchmarks, quarterly performance reviews and annual recertification, and proactive client communication for any performance issues.

Tier 2: Substantial Oversight

Tier 2 models require significant governance attention but with somewhat reduced intensity compared to Tier 1. These models typically warrant independent validation using standard approaches, complete development and validation documentation, regular performance monitoring with periodic reviews, and annual recertification with semi-annual reviews.

A market data interpolation model using cubic spline techniques for constructing yield curves exemplifies Tier 2 classification. The model has high materiality because it affects all fixed income valuations, but medium complexity as it employs well-established mathematical techniques with known properties.

Appropriate governance includes independent validation using standard curve construction benchmarks, complete documentation of interpolation methodology and validation results, daily monitoring of curve smoothness and economic reasonableness, semi-annual reviews and annual recertification, and client notification for significant curve construction issues.

Tier 3: Moderate Oversight

Tier 3 models warrant streamlined governance focusing on key risk areas without excessive bureaucracy. These models typically require streamlined validation focusing on essential risk areas, essential development and validation documentation, basic performance monitoring with exception reporting, and biennial recertification with annual reviews.

Simple aggregation and weighting calculations for client reporting represent typical Tier 3 models. These have low materiality because they are informational only and not used for risk decisions, combined with low complexity involving basic arithmetic operations. Appropriate governance includes streamlined validation focusing on calculation accuracy, essential documentation of calculation methodology, exception-based monitoring for obvious errors, annual reviews with biennial recertification, and client communication only for calculation errors affecting reports.

Tier 4: Minimal Oversight

Tier 4 models require only basic governance frameworks, recognising that excessive oversight would waste resources without meaningful risk reduction. These models typically warrant basic validation or acceptance of vendor validation, minimal documentation requirements, exception-based monitoring only, and triennial recertification or exception-based reviews.

Simple percentage calculations displayed in user interfaces exemplify Tier 4 classification. These have minimal materiality for display purposes only and low complexity involving basic percentage calculations. Minimal governance includes basic testing to ensure calculation accuracy, minimal documentation of calculation logic, no ongoing monitoring requirements, triennial review or exception-based recertification, and no specific client communication requirements.

The most common mistake vendors make is over-engineering governance for low-risk models. This occurs when Tier 1 governance requirements are applied to Tier 3 or 4 models, resulting in wasted resources that could be allocated to higher-risk models, delayed implementation, unnecessary complexity, reduced agility in low-risk model development, and client frustration with bureaucratic processes.

The opposite mistake—under-investing in high-risk models—proves equally damaging. Applying minimal governance to models that should be Tier 1 or 2 increases the probability of model failures affecting critical business functions, creates regulatory criticism during examinations, damages client confidence and potential contract losses, and causes operational failures and reputation damage.

Successful proportionality implementation requires vendors to develop their specific classification criteria that work for their particular business model and client base. This isn't a one-off exercise lifted from regulatory guidance or industry templates—it demands honest self-assessment of what materiality and complexity mean for your models and clients.

Complexity criteria require similar customisation as it depends on the sophistication and model savviness of the leadership team. The number of input variables that define "high complexity" for a pension fund analytics vendor differs significantly from that of a derivatives pricing vendor. Mathematical sophistication requirements, validation difficulty, and computational demands must align with your organisation's capabilities and constraints.

The critical requirement is continuous questioning and refinement. Those charged with developing the model risk framework must demonstrate ongoing "navel gazing"—constantly challenging whether their criteria work in practice rather than simply appearing theoretically elegant. Do the Tier 1 models receive the governance attention they deserve? Are Tier 4 models genuinely low-risk, or has the business evolved in ways that increase their importance?

This continuous questioning creates an effective feedback loop where monitoring results inform model tiering decisions, refining classification criteria. The framework becomes a living system that adapts to business changes rather than a static compliance exercise.

Governance templates scaled to each tier enable consistent application of proportionate standards. Documentation templates should reflect tier requirements, validation checklists should be appropriate for each complexity level, monitoring frameworks should be proportionate to materiality, and review schedules should align with risk levels.

Regular monitoring and adjustment ensure proportionality remains effective. Key questions include whether high-risk models are receiving adequate oversight, whether low-risk models are being over-engineered, whether clients accept and appreciate the proportionate approach, and whether governance resources are being allocated efficiently.

PROPORTIONALITY PROVIDES THE FOUNDATION FOR ALL SUBSEQUENT MODEL GOVERNANCE ACTIVITIES.

As we continue exploring practical implementation approaches, remember that every decision should be filtered through the proportionality lens:

"ARE WE IN CONTROL? IS THIS GOVERNANCE ACTIVITY PROPORTIONATE AND HENCE APPROPRIATE FOR THE MODEL'S RISK AND BUSINESS ACTIVITIES AND REVENUES THEY SUPPORT?"

9

LET'S GET MONITORING

Model monitoring involves regularly checking if your models are still performing as expected. The worst approach to model risk management is to wait for the annual validation process, during which the model is neglected.

REGULAR MONITORING SHIFTS THE FOCUS FROM A SINGLE SNAPSHOT TO IDENTIFYING TRENDS.

Trends are valuable for a model risk manager because early detection of issues is crucial. A senior risk officer told me this at the start of my risk career.

"EVERY ASPECT AND BRANCH OF RISK MANAGEMENT CAN BE BOILED DOWN TO NO SURPRISES. NOBODY SENIOR IN BANKING WELCOMES A SURPRISE".

The good news is that effective monitoring naturally builds from the model weaknesses and limitations discussed earlier. Those weren't academic exercises—they're your roadmap for what to watch. Each declared limitation suggests something specific to monitor.

The most effective monitoring frameworks begin with straightforward questions: "What could go wrong with this model, and how would we notice?" This isn't about building elaborate surveillance systems immediately. It's about establishing basic checks that warn early when models drift from their expected behaviour.

For most vendors, monitoring starts with the obvious metrics. If your model produces prices, track whether those prices remain reasonable compared to market benchmarks. If it calculates risk measures, watch for sudden spikes or drops that don't align with market conditions. These simple checks catch more problems than you might expect.

THE BEAUTY OF STARTING SIMPLE IS THAT IT BUILDS CONFIDENCE WITH MINIMAL UPFRONT INVESTMENT.

When banking validators see evidence that a vendor is systematically watching your models, even basic monitoring, demonstrates the right mindset. Start with the basics and enhance sophistication over time.

There are a few core types of monitoring worth considering:-

- **Size monitoring** is the simple equivalent of "trades/transactions," "notional" within an asset management perspective, or "delta" if derivatives are involved. It also includes the number of calls if the models sit behind an API.

- **Performance monitoring** evaluates how effectively the model fulfils its intended purpose. This involves observing whether predicted default rates match actual defaults for a credit scoring model. A pricing model includes comparing model prices to market prices or transaction levels.

- **Stability monitoring** ensures the model behaves consistently over time. This doesn't mean outputs never change—markets move, and model outputs should reflect those movements. Instead, it means watching for erratic behaviour, sudden shifts in model sensitivity, or outputs that become disconnected from underlying inputs.

• **Usage monitoring** confirms the model is being applied within its intended boundaries. This becomes particularly important when models are embedded in client systems, where you have limited visibility of their use. Simple usage statistics often reveal when applications have drifted beyond the model's validated scope.

• **Threshold monitoring** establishes acceptable ranges for key model outputs or performance metrics. When values fall outside these ranges, automated alerts trigger an investigation. The key is setting thresholds that balance sensitivity (catching real problems) with specificity (avoiding false alarms).

• **Comparison monitoring** benchmarks model outputs against alternative approaches, market data, or peer models. This provides context for assessing whether model behaviour reflects genuine market conditions or model-specific issues.

• **Operational monitoring,** especially reviewing operational logs for evidence of issues with running jobs and manual overrides.

The monitoring framework should reflect your model's tier classification. Tier 1 models deserve comprehensive monitoring with automated alerts and regular reporting. Tier 4 models only need exception-based monitoring that flags obvious problems.

Effective monitoring becomes part of normal operations rather than a special activity that requires additional effort. The best frameworks integrate monitoring into existing processes—monthly model review meetings, quarterly business reviews, or routine production support activities.

MANY VENDORS DISCOVER THAT MONITORING ACTIVITIES IMPROVE THEIR UNDERSTANDING OF HOW MODELS ACTUALLY PERFORM IN PRACTICE.

Academic validation tells you whether a model works in theory; operational monitoring reveals how it behaves when faced with real data, real users, and real business pressures.

There are not many mathematical jokes in the world, but it is worth noting that out of humanity, 3 out of 2 people struggle with fractions. This quote, however, makes a point:-

> *"THAT'S ALL VERY WELL, IT WORKS IN REALITY, BUT DOES IT WORK IN THEORY?"*

Model owners need to listen to what is working in practice and be in the loop regarding operational issues.

Consider the inflation bond market disruption of 2021[6]. Traditional curve fitting algorithms that had worked reliably for years suddenly started producing nonsensical results. The first sign wasn't a formal performance metric—it was operators having to repeatedly rerun curve construction jobs and manually adjust parameters to get reasonable outputs.

Similarly, during the 2009[7] low-rates-high-volatility environment, SABR swaption models began requiring constant manual calibration adjustments that had previously been rare exceptions.

These operational indicators overlap with operational risk management, but from a model risk perspective. When the same model component repeatedly requires manual intervention, or when override frequencies increase beyond normal patterns, it's time to investigate - and document - whether the model's underlying assumptions remain valid.

---

[6] https://en.wikipedia.org/wiki/2021%E2%80%932023_inflation_surge

[7] https://www.risk.net/sites/default/files/import_unmanaged/risk.net/data/asiarisk/pdf/2009/asiarisk_feb09_cuttingedge.pdf

Models exist in complex environments where multiple factors influence performance, and mechanically applying monitoring rules often misses important context.

The most effective monitoring combines automated data collection with regular human review. Technology handles the routine measurement and alerting; people interpret results, investigate anomalies, and decide whether observed changes require action.

When monitoring flags potential issues, the response should be proportionate to the problem's severity and the model's importance. Minor performance degradation in a low-risk model might warrant investigation but not immediate action. Significant problems with high-risk models demand urgent attention and potentially immediate model restrictions.

THE KEY IS HAVING CLEAR ESCALATION PROCEDURES THAT SPECIFY WHO GETS INVOLVED WHEN DIFFERENT TYPES OF PROBLEMS ARISE.

Model owners need to understand when they can resolve issues independently and when to escalate to senior management or notify clients.

Even basic monitoring gradually builds confidence. Each month of clean monitoring results proves that models are performing as expected. When problems do occur, a well-documented monitoring history helps differentiate genuine issues from normal variation.

This accumulated evidence becomes particularly valuable during model validation discussions. Rather than defending model quality based purely on development-phase testing, you can point to months or years of production monitoring demonstrating consistent performance.

The role of the model owner and their interaction with operations deserves a chapter on the operating model.

10

THE RACI IS ON!

When models start misbehaving, clarity about who does what becomes essential. The difference between a minor hiccup and a major crisis often comes down to whether everyone knows their role and can act decisively without lengthy email chains or committee discussions.

The RACI framework—Responsible, Accountable, Consulted, Informed—offers a practical structure for organising these roles. It is not just bureaucratic theory; it aims to ensure that when a model issue arises, the person receiving the alert knows exactly what they can decide independently and when they need to escalate.

Model ownership sits at the heart of any effective operating model. The model owner is accountable for the model's performance and appropriate use, but this doesn't mean they handle every operational task personally. Instead, they ensure that someone capable is responsible for each aspect of model operation and that appropriate oversight mechanisms exist.

This distinction is essential because model owners are usually quantitative professionals who understand the mathematical foundations and limitations of the model. While they may not be the appropriate individuals to restart failed production jobs or adjust system settings, they are the right people to determine whether unusual model behaviour requires immediate restrictions or can be postponed for further investigation.

Before we get into the details, here is the overview of the RACI model:-

Activity/Role	Operations Lead	Model Owner	Other Model Owners	Leadership Team
Routine Production Operations	R	A	I	I
Model Performance Monitoring	R	A	C	I
Standard Parameter Adjustments	R	A	I	I
Error Handling Procedures	R	A	I	I
Model Result Validation	C	A	C	I
Escalation of Model Issues	R	A	C	I
Model Restrictions/ Suspensions	C	A	C	I
Model Risk Tiering Decisions	I	C	A	I
Crisis Response Coordination	R	A	C	I
Client Communication	C	R	C	A
Regulatory Reporting	C	R	C	A
Post-Incident Reviews	C	A	C	I

The RACI model for a model in operation is as follows:-

• **Operations Lead** is responsible for the smooth running of the model-related jobs in production.

- **Model Owner** is accountable for the overall outcome of the production results.

- **Other Model Owners** are consulted on model-related issues and model risk Tiering.

- **Leadership Team** and other stakeholders, such as the audit and clients, are informed of material matters.

The key is defining clear boundaries around what operational teams can handle independently versus when they must involve model owners. Routine production issues—rerunning jobs with corrected data, applying standard parameter adjustments, or following established error-handling procedures—can typically be resolved operationally.

However, when models produce results that fall outside normal ranges, automated calibration fails repeatedly, or manual overrides become frequent, escalation to model owners becomes necessary. These operational indicators often provide the earliest warning that models are encountering conditions they weren't designed to handle.

Effective asset control requires documentation of standard operating procedures, including normal parameter ranges, acceptable override frequencies, and clear escalation triggers. This documentation serves as both operational guidance and evidence of systematic oversight for validation purposes.

The consultation network becomes particularly valuable during market dislocations when multiple models may be affected simultaneously. Rather than each model owner investigating issues independently, consultation mechanisms enable coordinated response and shared understanding of market-wide issues.

THE KEY IS MAKING CONSULTATION EFFICIENT RATHER THAN BUREAUCRATIC.

Pre-established communication channels, regular model owner meetings, and shared monitoring dashboards help ensure that relevant expertise can be accessed quickly when needed.

The "Informed" category encompasses stakeholders who need visibility into model issues without direct involvement in resolution. This typically includes senior management, client relationship managers, and oversight committees.

Information flow serves two purposes: enabling appropriate escalation when issues become material, and maintaining confidence through transparent communication about model oversight activities.

Regular reporting should distinguish between routine operational issues and genuine model performance problems. Stakeholders need to understand when models are operating normally despite operational complexity versus when model behaviour itself is concerning.

Client communication requires particular attention. Banking clients appreciate transparency about model oversight activities but need contextual information. A temporary increase in manual overrides during volatile market conditions tells a different story than the same increase during stable periods.

The operating model's real test comes during model failures or unusual market conditions.

"WHEN MODELS START PRODUCING QUESTIONABLE RESULTS, CLEAR ROLES ENABLE RAPID RESPONSE WITHOUT CONFUSION ABOUT DECISION-MAKING AUTHORITY. THE PLAY BOOK IS THE KEY - A FULLY DOCUMENTED AND REHEARSED SET OF RESPONSES TO EVENTS SUCH AS MODEL FAILURE"

Model owners must be empowered to impose immediate restrictions on model use while investigating problems. This might mean suspending automated processes, requiring manual review of all outputs, or temporarily reverting to alternative approaches. These decisions require authority commensurate with accountability.

Operational teams need explicit guidance on what defines a crisis that requires immediate escalation versus what can be managed through routine procedures. Time-sensitive environments require operational staff to recognise when model behaviour exceeds normal variation.

The consultation network enables rapid mobilisation of expertise when complex issues arise. Pre-established escalation procedures ensure appropriate technical and business expertise can be engaged quickly without bureaucratic delays.

Operating models improve through experience. Regularly reviewing how issues were handled reveals opportunities to refine roles, improve procedures, or enhance communication mechanisms.

Post-incident reviews should examine not just technical model performance but also operational effectiveness. Did escalation happen appropriately? Were the right people involved? Could faster resolution have been achieved with different procedures?

The operating model must be documented sufficiently to demonstrate systematic oversight to validation teams and regulators. This includes clear role definitions, escalation procedures, and evidence that the framework operates as designed.

The most sophisticated RACI frameworks fail if they don't work in practice. Implementation requires attention to practical details like communication channels, availability requirements, and backup arrangements for key roles.

Model owners need sufficient technical support to fulfil their accountability without becoming operational bottlenecks. This might involve deputy arrangements, shared decision-making protocols, or enhanced technical training for operational teams.

Operational teams require clear authority to act within specified boundaries and effective escalation mechanisms for when necessary. This demands real-time communication capabilities and well-defined escalation criteria.

Most importantly, clear operating models improve outcomes during genuine model issues. When everyone knows their role and can act within the defined authority, problems get resolved faster and with less business disruption.

The goal isn't perfect procedures but practical clarity that enables effective action when models need attention. The RACI framework provides structure, but success depends on adapting that structure to your specific business model and operational realities.

Now that we have an operating model, we can bring everything together to the Model Risk Committee.

11

MODEL RISK COMMITTEE

The Model Risk Committee (MRC) serves as the central nervous system of vendor model governance. It provides the forum for escalation, the authority for decision-making, and the accountability structure that clients and regulators expect.

MORE IMPORTANTLY, AN EFFECTIVE MRC TRANSFORMS MODEL GOVERNANCE FROM A COMPLIANCE BURDEN INTO A STRATEGIC CAPABILITY THAT IMPROVES MODEL QUALITY AND STRENGTHENS CLIENT RELATIONSHIPS.

The MRC operates under the leadership team's mandate and serves as both a decision-making body and an escalation forum for model risk management issues. Unlike internal audit functions or compliance committees, the MRC focuses specifically on the technical and business risks associated with models used in client-facing applications. Here is a quote I have often used to explain the MRC's purpose.

"A MODEL RISK COMMITTEE (MRC) IS A RISK-BASED FUNCTION, WHICH MEANS IT IS NOT A TALKING SHOP. THE MRC REVIEWS THE ARTEFACTS PROVIDED BY THE MODEL RISK GOVERNANCE PROCESS THAT THEY MANDATED, ASKS WHETHER THE OVERALL MODEL RISK IS APPROPRIATE FOR THE ENTERPRISE, AND ESCALATES TO THE LEADERSHIP GROUP WHEN IT IS NOT."

Here is an overview diagram of the MRC and the artefacts the members are responsible for:-

MODEL RISK COMMITTEE

Ownership of overall model risk
Risk-based Committee
Applies Proportional oversight
Provides model approval
Owns model framework

Ownership for each model
Owns the interoperable model risk
Collective responsibility
Evidence of challenge
Escalation to the ELT

STANDARDS

A single set of standards spanning the end-to-end lifecycle, aligned with SR 11-7

TEMPLATES

A single set of templates spanning the end-to-end lifecycle directly aligned to SR11-7

ARTEFACTS

Model Validation
Model Interoperability (string of peals)
Terms of Reference
Model Guidance
Monitoring Reports
Committee Minutes

Now that we know it is a risk committee that has mandated responsibility for a vendor's model risk, the MRC is also responsible for:-

- **Model Inventory.** Defining the distinct models within the organisation and at what level of granularity is appropriate.

- **Model Ownership:** Allocation of model owners to each model.

- **Model Tiering Signoff:** All model tiering decisions are brought to the MRC for explicit and minuted sign-off.

- **Template Definition:** The MRC enforces model governance standards across the organisation by creating templates, with examples in the appendix.

- **Policy Oversight:** The committee reviews and recommends approval of governance policies, including changes necessitated by regulatory developments, business growth, or lessons learned from implementation experience.

- **Approval Authority:** The MRC approves significant model changes, new model implementations, and material modifications to existing governance procedures.

- **Risk Assessment:** The committee regularly reviews key model risk metrics and reports, identifying trends and potential issues before they impact client operations.

- **Artefacts Retention.** Inclusion of the MRC terms of reference, policy documents, model validation work, templates, model inventory, MRC minutes and audit reviews.

- **Escalation Management:** The MRC provides a structured forum for escalating model performance issues, validation concerns, and implementation challenges that cannot be resolved at the operational level.

The MRC should have the following voting members:-

- The MRC Chairman should possess technical credibility and organisational authority and act as the single escalation point.

- Model Owners are responsible for each model or model category. They bring intimate knowledge of model design, implementation, and operational performance.

- A Leadership Team representative who can be the senior Auditor, Legal Counsel or a division head.

Other non-voting members or those invited would include operations, finance and audit.

The most critical function of the MRC is demonstrating genuine "effective challenge"—not just rubber-stamping model owner recommendations or conducting perfunctory reviews. Banking validators and regulators look specifically for evidence that model decisions have been questioned, alternatives considered, and assumptions tested by qualified professionals who weren't involved in the original model development.

This challenge must be real, documented, and visible in committee minutes. Empty phrases like "the committee discussed the model" provide no evidence of challenge; specific questions, alternative viewpoints, and follow-up actions demonstrate that rigorous scrutiny occurred. The MRC minutes become the audited record that the organisation takes model risk seriously and subjects its models to independent review.

An effective challenge emerges through preparation, expertise, and a cultural commitment (not easy) to asking uncomfortable questions. It is not personal; as we said earlier, not all models are wrong, but some can be useful.

Model owners must present their work openly and constructively, including limitations and uncertainties, while committee members must come prepared to probe assumptions and challenge conclusions. This isn't adversarial—it's protective.

The goal of the MRC is to take collective responsibility in identifying potential problems before they affect clients. When model performance later deteriorates or market conditions expose model weaknesses, this documented challenge history demonstrates that the

Model development activities must follow structured methodologies that ensure the analytical solution's transparency, reproducibility, and maintainability. The development process begins with comprehensive documentation of the conceptual framework, including detailed assessments of alternative methodologies, clear articulation of assumptions and limitations, and explicit justification for the chosen analytical approach.

This documentation serves multiple purposes beyond immediate development needs—it provides the foundation for validation activities, enables future model enhancements, and supports regulatory examinations or audit reviews. The MRC provides oversight during this phase, monitoring development progress against established timelines and ensuring adherence to governance standards while respecting the development team's technical autonomy.

Peer code review is a critical quality control mechanism within the development process. It provides an independent assessment of methodology implementation, code quality, and analytical soundness before models progress to formal validation.

Effective peer review involves experienced practitioners who can evaluate the solution's technical implementation and conceptual appropriateness, identifying potential issues such as coding errors, inappropriate assumptions, or methodological weaknesses.

This review process often prevents significant issues from emerging during later validation phases, reducing overall development timelines and improving model quality. The peer review should encompass the core analytical components, data handling procedures, error checking mechanisms, and documentation completeness.

Functional testing forms the final component of the development stage, verifying that the model produces expected results under various scenarios and operates reliably within its intended operating environment. This testing extends beyond simple accuracy checks, including stress testing under extreme conditions, validation of edge case handling, and confirmation that the model behaves appropriately when subjected to unusual or corrupted input data.

The testing framework should document all test scenarios, expected outcomes, and results, creating an evidence base supporting subsequent validation activities.

The MRC maintains oversight throughout the development process, ensuring that quality gates are met before progression to validation while avoiding stepping on the toes of development teams, which retain responsibility for technical execution and delivery against agreed-upon specifications.

The "Validate Model" stage represents the independent assessment phase, where:

VALIDATION IS WHEN A QUALIFIED PRACTITIONER EVALUATES WHETHER THE DEVELOPED MODEL MEETS ITS INTENDED PURPOSE AND OPERATES WITHIN ACCEPTABLE RISK PARAMETERS.

For most regulated financial institutions, this function is well-established with dedicated model validation teams, but the principles remain applicable across all organisations using quantitative models for business-critical decisions.

This stage provides essential independent challenge by evaluating model choice decisions, implementation, and performance characteristics. SR 11-7 compliance forms the regulatory backbone for financial institutions, establishing that models must demonstrate they "do what they say on the tin" through rigorous testing of accuracy, stability, and appropriate usage under various conditions.

The validation process begins with a documentation review, examining the business rationale, methodology approach, and known weaknesses identified during development. This review extends beyond technical assessment to include evaluation of model ownership, change history, and alignment with organisational risk appetite. Validators must independently verify that development documentation adequately supports the model's intended application and that all assumptions are clearly articulated and justified.

Data validation is critical, focusing on the adequacy, representativeness, and quality of datasets used for model development and testing. This includes assessment of lookback periods, sample granularity, portfolio applicability, and treatment of outliers or missing data. The validation team must satisfy itself that the underlying data appropriately reflects the population and time horizon for which the model will be applied, identifying any gaps or biases that could compromise model performance.

Methodology review involves a detailed examination of the conceptual approach, comparison with alternative methodologies, and assessment of assumptions and limitations. Validators evaluate whether the chosen methodology represents industry best practice, whether simplifications are appropriate, and whether the mathematical formulation correctly implements the intended approach. This review includes stress testing model behaviour under extreme conditions and evaluating cross-term dynamics that could affect model stability.

Evidence challenge forms the final validation component, where findings are documented, remediation plans developed, and overall risk ratings assigned.

Evidence challenge forms the final validation component, where findings are documented, remediation plans developed, and overall risk ratings assigned. For organisations without dedicated validation teams, the model owner can complete validation documentation with independent review by another qualified model owner before formal MRC assessment.

The model owner must propose an appropriate risk tier based on the model's complexity and materiality. The MRC receives validation findings and the proposed risk tier, overseeing the resolution of identified issues before approving the model's progression to production. The MRC also ensures that any conditions of use or ongoing monitoring requirements are clearly established and communicated to model users, the audit, and the leadership team.

The "Implement in Production" stage is the critical handover between quants and technology:

IMPLEMENTING INTO PRODUCTION IS THE CRITICAL TRANSITION WHERE VALIDATED MODELS MOVE FROM CONTROLLED DEVELOPMENT ENVIRONMENTS TO PRODUCTION ENVIRONMENTS.

This phase typically falls under the responsibility of technology teams and business implementation specialists who manage the complex process of integrating analytical solutions with existing infrastructure, data feeds, and user interfaces.

This area operates under established change management and deployment protocols for most organisations, with dedicated project management and technical implementation teams leading the effort. The model owner and MRC function primarily as observers during this stage, monitoring the implementation process to ensure the model performs as expected when integrated with production systems and data feeds.

Integration testing forms the cornerstone of this stage, validating that the model operates correctly within the broader technology ecosystem. This testing encompasses system interfaces, data flow validation, user access controls, and performance under production-level data volumes. The testing framework must verify that the analytical logic developed in isolation continues to function accurately when embedded within complex technological environments, including validation of calculation engines, data transformation processes, and output formatting requirements.

Data feed testing ensures that production data sources provide the expected quality, format, and timeliness required for model operation.

This includes validation of data extraction processes, transformation logic, and error handling mechanisms when data quality issues arise. Testing must cover normal operating conditions as well as edge cases such as missing data, delayed feeds, or corrupted input files. The model owner observes this testing to confirm that data handling aligns with assumptions made during the development and validation phases.

Regression testing provides confidence that the production implementation produces results consistent with the validated model. This involves comparing production outputs with benchmark results from the validation environment, ensuring that no unintended changes occurred during the implementation process.

The MRC maintains oversight of regression testing results, requiring satisfactory reconciliation before final approval for the model to be used in production. Where significant discrepancies emerge between the model in development and the model instance in production, the MRC may require additional investigation or remediation before permitting full deployment, ensuring that model integrity is preserved throughout the implementation process.

The "Monitor Performance" stage is the follow-up suite of processes to support the model in production.

MODEL MONITORING ENCOMPASSES THE ONGOING OVERSIGHT ACTIVITIES THAT ENSURE MODELS OPERATE EFFECTIVELY THROUGHOUT THEIR OPERATIONAL LIFECYCLE.

As discussed in previous chapters, comprehensive monitoring frameworks are essential for detecting model degradation, data quality issues, and changes in underlying market conditions that could affect model reliability. The monitoring requirements established during validation must now be integrated into the organisation's operational framework, with clear responsibilities, escalation procedures, and remediation protocols.

Model owners often lack the operational discipline required for consistent monitoring execution, making it essential to embed these activities within established business processes through a clear RACI framework.

Operational teams typically have the systems and processes to execute regular checks and are responsible for day-to-day monitoring. At the same time, the model owner remains accountable for performance outcomes and must respond to identified issues.

The MRC provides consultation on monitoring standards and receives information on model performance trends, while key stakeholders across the business are informed of any material changes in model behaviour. This structured approach ensures monitoring becomes a sustainable operational capability rather than a discretionary activity dependent on individual model owners' attention and availability.

The "Manage Model Risk" stage combines model validation and model monitoring.

MODEL RISK MANAGEMENT ENCOMPASSES THE ONGOING GOVERNANCE ACTIVITIES THAT OVERSEE MODEL RISKS THROUGHOUT THEIR OPERATIONAL LIFECYCLE.

As established earlier, the MRC provides central oversight of model risk management, including risk appetite assessment, evaluation of remediation plans, and decisions regarding model decommissioning.

When models exhibit deteriorating performance, data quality issues, or changed business requirements, the MRC evaluates whether remediation efforts are sufficient or whether model retirement is necessary.

These decisions account for not only technical factors but also business impact, regulatory requirements, and resource constraints, ensuring that model risk management remains aligned with organisational objectives and risk tolerance.

The "Model Inventory" represents the central repository.

MODEL INVENTORY MAINTAINS COMPREHENSIVE RECORDS OF ALL MODELS THROUGHOUT THEIR LIFECYCLE, SERVING AS THE AUTHORITATIVE SOURCE FOR MODEL GOVERNANCE INFORMATION.

This system captures essential metadata, including model identification, purpose, technical specifications, ownership details, and current status within the governance framework. Beyond basic cataloguing, the inventory tracks lifecycle management activities from development through retirement, maintaining links to validation documentation, deployment records, and performance monitoring data.

Integration interfaces enable automated data ingestion from development environments and real-time synchronisation with production systems, ensuring the inventory remains current without relying on manual updates.

The inventory incorporates robust access controls and workflow engines that support governance processes through automated approval chains, compliance alerts, and reporting dashboards. This infrastructure enables the MRC to oversee the complete model portfolio, identify models requiring attention, track remediation progress, and ensure that governance standards are consistently applied across all model instances.

Rather than functioning as a static catalogue, the model inventory becomes an active component of the risk management framework, providing the information architecture necessary for effective model governance at enterprise scale.

The model risk lifecycle provides a structured framework for managing quantitative models from initial conception through eventual decommissioning. It ensures that each stage builds upon the previous while maintaining governance oversight throughout the model's life.

The six interconnected stages—defining the business case, developing the model, validation, production implementation, performance monitoring, and risk management—create a comprehensive approach that balances business innovation with operational risk control.

Central to this framework is the recognition that effective model governance requires clear delineation of responsibilities, with the MRC serving as an advisory and oversight function while respecting the technical autonomy of development teams and the strategic authority of business sponsors. The model inventory underpins this entire lifecycle, providing the information infrastructure necessary for enterprise-scale sustainable governance. Organisations implementing this lifecycle approach typically experience improved model quality, reduced operational risk, and enhanced regulatory compliance, while maintaining the agility necessary to respond to evolving business requirements and market conditions.

13

PRODUCT VALUATION MODEL

The journey from model development to production deployment represents one of the most critical transitions in model risk management—the moment when theoretical elegance meets operational reality. While previous chapters focused on models as analytical methodologies, requiring governance and validation, this chapter addresses what happens when those models become embedded within the production systems.

In banking operations, practitioners often use the terms "model" and "product" interchangeably, given that there is usually a one-to-one relationship between product and model. This simplification creates confusion and overlooks the difference between a model built in a safe environment and those in production. To this end, we introduce the concept of a Product Valuation Model. Here is its definition:

A PRODUCT VALUATION MODEL (PVM), HOWEVER, REPRESENTS SOMETHING FUNDAMENTALLY DIFFERENT –THE INSTANCE OF A MODEL WITHIN A PRODUCTION ENVIRONMENT WHERE IT MUST INTERACT WITH REAL MARKET DATA, COMPUTATIONAL INFRASTRUCTURE, AND BUSINESS PROCESSES.

This distinction matters enormously for risk management. A sophisticated pricing model that performs flawlessly in a controlled development environment may behave quite differently when subjected to production systems' constraints, data quality issues, and computational limitations.

With the migration of instrument valuation models into production with live portfolios, we can now extend the MRC coverage to defining the taxonomy and monitoring under the framework of PVM, which addresses the real-life issues concerning the production of valuations, sensitivities, and stress results.

This extension signifies a natural progression in model risk management beyond the development and validation stages. While traditional model governance concentrates on ensuring analytical robustness and correct implementation, PVM governance and the RACI operating model recognise that additional risks arise when models operate within live trading environments, processing real portfolio data and supporting genuine business decisions.

An individual PVM defines the pairing of a Product ID instance with a unique combination of the following components, each contributing its own risk characteristics to the overall system:

- **Market Data Model** - The systematic approach to sourcing, processing, and transforming market information into the specific data inputs required by analytical models (e.g. ICE direct, curve interpolation/extrapolation). This encompasses data vendors, curve construction methodologies, proxy relationships for missing data points, and the timing and frequency of data updates.

- **Analytical Model**—This is the core quantitative methodology that has undergone the development and validation processes described in previous chapters (e.g., Bond/cashflow, Black Scholes). This mathematical engine applies theoretical frameworks to produce valuations, risk measures, and sensitivities.

- **Calculating Engine** - The technological platform responsible for executing calculations, managing computational resources, handling data flows, and delivering results to end users (e.g. Calypso, AM). This includes both software applications and the underlying infrastructure supporting model execution.

A PVM for a product that is a Government Bond and an Equity Option would look like this:

- NSSF_bond_curve.Bond_Pricer.Murex.
- NSS_equity_vol.Black_Scholes.Murex
- SABR_swaption_vol.Black_Scholes.Murex

This PVM identifier tells us that the system uses a specific bond curve construction methodology (Market Data Model), applies a particular bond pricing algorithm (Analytics Model), and executes these calculations within the Murex platform (Computation Engine). Each component introduces its own assumptions, limitations, and potential failure modes that must be understood and managed. The NSSF refers to the Nelson-Siegel-Svensson curve fitting tool with a filtered subset of available bonds.

One notable challenge faced by models in production environments is balancing analytical sophistication with operational timeliness. This challenge is most evident during overnight batch processing windows, where complex valuation runs must finish before the market opens the next day. The role of MRC is to oversee the harsh reality of computational limitations and manual workarounds.

The classic example is Monte Carlo simulations, which rely on iterative random sampling to produce convergent results. During model development and validation, these simulations might run with 50,000 or 100,000 iterations to ensure statistical robustness and smooth convergence. However, when embedded within production PVMs processing thousands of instruments across multiple portfolios, such computational intensity becomes operationally untenable, leading to lower iterations that create unwanted noise for the trader.

All calibration processes that involve goal-seeking algorithms suffer from similar timing pressures. Yield curve construction, volatility surface fitting, and correlation matrix optimisation require iterative numerical methods that could theoretically run for hours to achieve perfect convergence. Production realities demand that these processes complete within minutes, forcing practitioners to accept "good enough" calibrations rather than optimal solutions.

The other aspect is the gradual staleness of input parameters that aren't updated frequently enough. Market data feeds capture prices and rates that change continuously, but many model parameters update far less frequently due to operational complexity or computational cost.

Correlation matrices exemplify this phenomenon, as there are few live markets in correlation swaps. Mean reversion parameters in interest rate and credit models face similar staleness issues. The infamous "Berm Tax" tracks the discount to what a Bermudian option trades at relative to a replicating portfolio. The final example is the CPR prepayment rate for an MBS. The list continues, but these are often hidden deep within production.

The Product Valuation Model framework provides the most effective approach to model monitoring, addressing a fundamental challenge that emerges in production environments: the same analytical model often supports multiple PVMs across different products, markets, and computational platforms. Traditional model-centric monitoring can miss critical risks that only become apparent at the PVM level.

Imagine a Black-Scholes pricing model that could be used across multiple PVMs, such as equities, forex, and commodities. Monitoring only at the model level could suggest that Black-Scholes performs adequately on average, but it might hide significant issues in particular PVM implementations.

A particularly insidious risk emerges when new products are "shoehorned" into existing models, usually inappropriately, leaving critical risks missing in action. This typically occurs when business pressures to launch new products quickly override proper model development and validation processes. Rather than developing appropriate analytical frameworks, new instruments get forced into the closest available model, often with inadequate consideration of the resulting risk profile.

For example, a barrier option might be valued using a standard Black-Scholes PVM simply because it is the only available equity pricing framework. The barrier features fundamentally change the risk characteristics, which are ignored or approximated through a static spread trade. The resulting PVM produces prices and sensitivities, but completely misses the critical barrier-related risks that should drive hedging decisions.

As mentioned several times in this handbook, the best approach with monitoring is to start with the basics and build up once such activity is bedded in:

- **Notional Outstanding** - Tracking the total notional amount processed through each PVM reveals business growth patterns, concentration risks, and potential model capacity issues. Sudden spikes in notional indicate new product launches that haven't been adequately validated, while gradual increases help identify when computational performance will become problematic.

- **Maturity Profile**—Monitoring the distribution of maturities across instruments in each PVM can reveal model appropriateness issues. For example, a PVM designed for short-dated instruments suddenly processing long-dated exposures might indicate shoehorning problems. Similarly, clustering around specific maturity dates might suggest operational conveniences that don't reflect genuine business requirements.

- **Key Sensitivities** - Tracking delta and vega provides insight into both model behaviour and portfolio risk characteristics. Sensitivities that become unstable, exhibit unusual patterns, or fail to respond appropriately to market movements often indicate underlying model problems that aren't apparent from price comparisons alone.

The most powerful validation of PVM performance comes through P&L backtesting, which compares the Hypothetical P&L calculated using Taylor's approximation with actual P&L results. This analysis creates the ultimate early warning system that a model is either not capturing changes in market conditions or missing risk entirely.

The process involves calculating what portfolio P&L should have been based on observed market moves and the model's sensitivities (delta and vega), then comparing this theoretical result against actual trading P&L. The difference between hypothetical and actual P&L provides direct evidence of model adequacy in real market conditions.

When models accurately capture portfolio risks, hypothetical P&L should closely track actual results. Significant unexplained differences indicate model problems that may not be apparent through other monitoring approaches. Persistent positive unexplained P&L suggests the model is underestimating risks, while persistent negative differences could indicate missing risk factors or inappropriate model applications.

This attribution analysis becomes particularly valuable at the PVM level because it connects model performance directly to business outcomes. It provides immediate, actionable insight into whether models are serving their fundamental purpose: accurately representing portfolio risks for business decision-making.

14

INTEROPERABILITY

Model interoperability represents one of the most complex challenges in modern financial institutions, where individual models rarely operate in isolation. Instead, they form intricate networks where the output of one model becomes the input to another, creating what practitioners often describe as a "string of pearls" arrangement. Each handover point in this chain introduces potential risks that can amplify across the entire system, making robust interoperability governance essential for maintaining system integrity.

Complexity arises not only from technical integration issues but also from fundamental differences in how models are designed, validated, and maintained. When models developed by different teams, using different methodologies, and potentially based on different assumptions, need to work together seamlessly, the risk of misalignment and error propagation increases significantly.

In any interoperability scenario, we can identify a clear provider-consumer relationship where one model (the provider) generates outputs that serve as inputs for another model (the consumer). This seemingly straightforward relationship becomes complex when we consider the multiple layers of assumptions, data transformations, and risk considerations that must align between the two systems.

The provider and consumer models operate under specific design assumptions about data quality, frequency, granularity, and acceptable use cases. The handover point becomes a critical junction where these potentially misaligned assumptions should be reconciled.

The most insidious challenge in model interoperability lies in an unstated assumption that pervades most provider-consumer relationships. Greg N. Gregoriou's book "Operational Risk Toward

Basel III: Best Practices and Issues in Modelling, Management, and Regulation" stated that:

THE CONSUMER MODEL ASSUMES THE PROVIDER'S DATA IS ERROR-FREE AND THE PROVIDER ASSUMES NO RESPONSIBILITY FOR COMMUNICATING DATA QUALITY ISSUES.

This creates a silent contract where crucial information about limitations, caveats, and uncertainties is systematically lost at each handover point.

Provider models, developed under specific constraints and assumptions, invariably make compromises—what might uncharitably be called "corner-cutting" for practical implementation. The provider model team understands these compromises well but rarely documents them in a way that downstream models can consume.

Meanwhile, while dealing with their practical pressures, downstream consumer models take shortcuts, often including the risky assumption that upstream data is reliable and complete.

When provider and consumer models make undocumented practical compromises, the cumulative effect becomes impossible to track. A provider model might use simplified risk factor correlations during volatile periods, while a consumer model might assume that input correlations are stable over time. Neither assumption is documented in a way that allows assessment of their combined impact.

One of the most significant risks in model interoperability lies in error amplification. Minor inaccuracies or biases in a provider model can compound as they flow through consumer models, particularly when multiple models are chained together. This compounding effect occurs through several mechanisms:

- **Statistical Compounding**: When models make sequential predictions based on previous model outputs, statistical errors can compound according to error propagation principles. A 2% error in a provider model might result in a 5% error in the final consumer model output after accounting for the consumer model's own uncertainties.

- **Bias Propagation:** Systematic biases in training data or model specification can propagate and amplify through interconnected systems. The classic example is a credit risk model that consistently underestimates default rates for a particular demographic.

- **Distributional Assumptions:** When provider and consumer models make different distributional assumptions about the same underlying phenomena, the handover process can introduce systematic distortions that amplify under stressed conditions.

- **Assumption Cascades:** Each model in a chain embeds assumptions about its inputs. The effects cascade through the entire model network when these assumptions are incorrect or invalid due to changing market conditions. A liquidity model assuming normal market conditions may provide inputs to a portfolio optimisation model that assumes those liquidity estimates remain valid during stress periods.

- **Confidence Inflation:** Consumer models often treat provider outputs as "ground truth" rather than estimates with associated uncertainty. This confidence inflation means that the final outputs appear more reliable than they are, potentially leading to inappropriate risk-taking or inadequate capital reserves.
Inconsistent Assumptions

Models developed by different teams or at different times often embed different assumptions about market behaviour, regulatory requirements, or business processes. These assumption differences create interoperability challenges that go beyond technical integration issues.

- **Temporal Misalignment:** Provider models may be based on historical market conditions or regulatory frameworks that have since evolved. Consumer models designed under current conditions may not appropriately handle outputs from models based on outdated assumptions.

- **Methodological Differences:** Different modelling teams may prefer various statistical methods, risk measures, or validation techniques. When a consumer model expecting outputs from a Value-at-Risk framework receives inputs from a model using Expected Shortfall, the methodological mismatch can cause inaccurate risk assessments.

- **Business Logic Variations:** Models created for various business units may incorporate different assumptions regarding customer behaviour, market dynamics, or operational constraints. These variations become problematic when models intended for different business contexts need to work together.

As data flows from provider to consumer models, it often undergoes compression or aggregation that can result in information loss. This compression occurs for several reasons: system limitations, different granularity requirements, or attempts to standardise interfaces between diverse systems.

- **Aggregation Effects:** When detailed provider outputs are aggregated for consumption by downstream models, important distributional information may be lost. A consumer model receiving average values may not understand the underlying variability that could be crucial for accurate risk assessment.

- **Dimensionality Reduction:** Downstream models may reduce Complex provider outputs to simplified summary statistics for consumption. This reduction can eliminate important correlation structures or tail risk information that could be material for consumer model accuracy.

- **Temporal Compression:** Provider models may operate at different time horizons than consumer models, requiring temporal aggregation or interpolation that can obscure important time-series patterns or volatility structures.

The interoperability challenges outlined above demonstrate why organisations benefit from having a Model Risk Committee (MRC) that can oversee the entire portfolio of model assets, including their interactions. Traditional governance frameworks focusing solely on individual models often overlook the risks inherent in model networks.

The MRC's role becomes especially crucial in understanding network-level risks that arise from model interactions. While individual models may perform well independently, their combination can exhibit poor performance due to incompatible assumptions or flawed handover mechanisms. This is why the MRC's portfolio-wide view is vital—it enables the organisation to identify and manage risks that span multiple models and business functions.

These issues become particularly acute when vendor models feed into a bank's capital or credit models. The model validation teams need visibility on the vendor model's assumptions and limitations within their risk and capital calculation context. This is a significant challenge for banks, and the vendor's MRC must understand how they are positioned within the bank's model ecosystem.

Suppose the model validators can see an equivalent function related to model risk governance that integrates with their templates. In that case, they are more willing to work with that vendor rather than one that merely responds to requests for information.

At this juncture, I mention the overlap between model interoperability and the regulation BCBS 239, which provides a set of principles to enforce transparency and traceability of how risk and reference data move through an organisation and end up in capital and risk disclosure.

For completeness, I have included an overview of BCBS 239 in the appendix in case it ever comes up in conversation.

15

THE AI PARADOX

As immortalised in the film Midnight Cowboy, "everyone is talkin' at AI, I don't hear a word they're sayin'". All companies—clients and vendors alike—are under pressure to get on board, unleash their data and experiment with AI.

Some want to enhance a product or service, others aim to cut staff or pursue ChatGPT-ification of their operations. Who knows the exact motivation, but avoiding anything is not an option. In this hyped-up world, enthusiasm and shiny new toy syndrome inevitably take hold.

The initial pilot projects often show remarkable promise. A credit scoring model demonstrates improved accuracy, a chatbot handles routine customer inquiries effectively, or a predictive maintenance system identifies equipment failures before they occur. The natural response is enthusiasm: if the hype is real and AI works this well in controlled circumstances, imagine what it could accomplish across the entire organisation?

However, this enthusiasm often becomes a strategic liability for vendors' clients. Research consistently shows that 75% of AI projects fail to meet expected returns, with failure rates rising rather than falling as organisations gain experience. The gap between pilot success and enterprise-wide failure isn't mainly about technology—it's about underestimating how internal and vendor AI solutions can be integrated into existing client processes.

This handbook covers the model risk governance framework, which provides an excellent foundation for AI governance with its time-tested tiered approach based on materiality and complexity.

The nine foundational questions from SR 11-7 capture the essence of model risk management, but AI models introduce additional considerations that warrant systematic attention. Rather than replacing these questions, we can extend them to address AI-specific risks while maintaining the elegant simplicity of the original framework.

Question 1: Does the model do what it says on the tin?

AI models, particularly deep learning systems, create internal representations that may not align with human understanding of the problem domain.

WHEN THE AI MODEL MAKES PREDICTIONS, CAN WE IDENTIFY WHICH FACTORS ARE DOMINANT AND HOW SENSITIVE THEY ARE TO THE RELEVANT DATA?

This doesn't require complete mathematical transparency—often impossible with complex neural networks—but vendors should consider providing some mechanism for understanding which inputs most strongly influence outputs.

The "Ronseal test" for AI also extends to behavioural consistency. Does the model behave predictably when presented with similar inputs? AI models may exhibit surprising discontinuities where small input changes produce large output changes. While this can sometimes reflect genuine insights about the underlying phenomenon, it more often indicates overfitting or instability that requires investigation.

Question 2: Does the model provide timely, accurate and stable results?

The issue of stability is particularly significant for AI models. Unlike traditional models, where stability primarily concerns computational performance, AI model stability has an additional layer.

For example, a traditional credit scoring model might have a clear rule: "If the debt-to-income ratio increases by 5%, decrease the score by 10 points." That's predictable and stable.

AN AI MODEL MIGHT LEARN COMPLEX PATTERNS THAT ARE NOT OBVIOUS TO THE USER AND COULD BE PHANTOM.

It might treat two loan applicants with nearly identical profiles very differently because it's picking up on subtle combinations of factors not easily seen or understood. Or worse, it might work perfectly for months and then suddenly start making different decisions for similar cases after it's been retrained with new data.

Additional considerations for AI systems: AI models can exhibit what researchers call "catastrophic forgetting"—when additional training on new data causes the model to lose previously learned capabilities. This creates a unique form of model risk where attempting to improve performance degrades it.

Governance frameworks should consider monitoring this phenomenon and establishing protocols for incremental learning that preserve existing capabilities.

Hallucination represents another stability challenge unique to AI systems. Language models may confidently generate plausible but factually incorrect information. For vendors, this means building in safeguards and providing clear guidance to clients about when and how these issues might manifest.

Questions 3-9: Enhanced Considerations for AI

The remaining foundational questions—covering industry standards, computational resources, technical debt, manual overrides, risk decision-making, model interconnections, limitations, monitoring requirements, and overall risk acceptability—all benefit from AI-specific enhancements.

INDUSTRY STANDARDS FOR AI REMAIN NASCENT AND EVOLVING. WHAT CONSTITUTES BEST PRACTICE FOR AI MODEL DEVELOPMENT CONTINUES TO EMERGE.

Vendors should consider staying current with rapidly evolving standards while recognising that today's best practices may prove inadequate tomorrow. As with much of the Model Risk Governance, start simple and build with experience.

Technical debt in AI systems can accumulate rapidly. The experimental nature of AI development often leads to shortcuts and workarounds that create maintainability challenges. Model versioning becomes critical as AI systems evolve through continuous learning. Dependencies on specific data sources, feature engineering pipelines, and preprocessing steps create complex webs of interconnection that traditional models rarely exhibit.

The traditional four-tier classification system works well for AI models, but each tier requires additional nuanced considerations that reflect AI-specific risks.

Tier 1 AI Models: Critical Decision Systems

Tier 1 AI models warrant the most comprehensive governance not just because of their materiality and complexity, but because they often operate in domains where the stakes of error extend beyond financial loss, including reputational damage, regulatory sanctions, and harm to individuals or communities.

A credit or a flood scoring AI model influencing lending decisions exemplifies Tier 1 classification. Beyond the traditional requirements for comprehensive validation and documentation, this model requires ongoing bias monitoring to ensure it doesn't inadvertently discriminate against protected classes.

The validation process should consider including fairness metrics alongside traditional performance measures. If the model exhibits disparate impact across demographic groups, the governance framework should consider protocols for investigating whether these differences reflect legitimate risk factors or problematic bias.

The key challenge for vendors is ensuring their AI solutions can integrate into the client's existing decision-making processes. For credit approval, the AI model output needs to be explainable to loan officers, auditable for compliance purposes, and compatible with the client's risk appetite and regulatory requirements. The vendor's documentation should address how the model fits into these broader decision workflows.

The monitoring requirements for Tier 1 AI models extend beyond performance tracking to include behavioural analysis. Does the model's decision-making process remain consistent over time? Are there emerging patterns that suggest drift in the underlying relationships the model has learned? These questions require new types of monitoring infrastructure that traditional models don't need, and vendors should consider providing tools and guidance for ongoing behavioural monitoring.

Documentation for Tier 1 AI models should address explainability requirements. While we can't always explain exactly how a neural network reaches its conclusions, vendors can document what factors it considers important, how it behaves across different types of inputs, and what limitations have been observed in its reasoning. This documentation serves both validation and practical purposes when human operators need to understand and potentially override AI recommendations.

Tier 2 and 3 AI Models: Proportionate Enhancements

Mid-tier AI models benefit from scaled versions of the enhanced governance controls. A customer service chatbot might warrant Tier 2 classification due to its customer-facing nature and moderate complexity. The governance requirements would include bias monitoring for sensitive customer interactions, hallucination detection to prevent the system from providing incorrect information, and escalation protocols for situations the AI cannot handle appropriately.

Tier 3 models, such as internal process automation tools, require lighter, meaningful enhancements. These include basic bias checking, simple hallucination monitoring, and exception reporting for unusual behaviours. The key principle remains proportionality—applying sophisticated controls where they add value while avoiding bureaucratic overhead for lower-risk applications.

The most honest acknowledgement we can make about AI governance is that we operate in uncharted territory. There are no universally agreed-upon best practices, comprehensive regulatory frameworks, or decades of experience to guide our decisions. This uncertainty doesn't excuse inaction—it demands thoughtful, risk-based approaches that can adapt as our understanding evolves.

The "effective challenge" risk management principle becomes even more important in this context. Vendors should consider developing governance frameworks that encourage questioning assumptions, testing boundaries, and learning from failures. The rapid pace of AI development means that today's cutting-edge techniques may become tomorrow's cautionary tales. Governance frameworks should embrace this uncertainty while still providing meaningful oversight.

This uncertainty also means that vendors should consider developing internal capabilities for AI risk assessment rather than relying entirely on external standards or client assurances. The questions we ask about AI models may need to evolve as quickly as the technology itself.

This continuous learning imperative extends beyond technical monitoring to understand how AI integrates with client processes. How effectively are human operators working with AI recommendations? Are there patterns in when humans choose to override AI suggestions? Do these override patterns reveal blind spots in the AI model or gaps in human understanding? Vendors should consider capturing and analysing these human-AI interaction patterns to improve the technology and the processes surrounding it.

The goal isn't to eliminate uncertainty or achieve perfect control over AI systems. Instead, it's to develop capabilities for working effectively with uncertain, evolving technologies while maintaining appropriate risk discipline.

AI governance represents an evolution of model risk management rather than a revolution. The foundational principles remain sound but require nuanced adaptation to address AI systems' unique characteristics.

By building on proven frameworks while remaining open to learning and adaptation, vendors can develop AI solutions that enable clients to realise the benefits of AI while effectively managing its risks.

16

GETTING STARTED

The first thing to do is not to panic. The evolution, including acceptance, of a model risk framework takes time, and every model validation function recognises your challenges. Model people don't get out much, so there is some sense of camaraderie amongst quants who live in an imperfect world.

To get started, you need to take a few key actions in the first three months, which will allow you to inform your banking clients about the shift in direction. The best approach is to consider this a 12-week cycle, with each week being a 5-day sprint towards your goals of a complete framework.

Imagine your largest banking client calling with an unexpected request: "We need to see your model governance framework." The following silence isn't uncommon—most vendors scramble to explain processes that don't formally exist. But this moment, rather than being a crisis, can become the catalyst for transformation.

In the first week, many vendor organisations discovered they operated with far more model risk than anyone had realised. That algorithmic trading model that's been running for three years? No one documented its limitations.

Banking validators are seasoned practitioners who have witnessed models fail dramatically during market stress. They seek evidence that you thoroughly understand your own creations enough to manage the risks they pose.

The most critical decision in your first month isn't technical—it's cultural. Does leadership genuinely understand that this transformation requires more than just checking regulatory boxes?

This is what a GANTT view of the project will look like:-

Activity	W1	W2	W3	W4	W5	W6	W7	W8	W9	W10	W11	W12
Leadership Training	X	X										
Written Mandate	X	X										
Staff Communication		X	X									
Model Inventory			X	X								
Model Owner Assignment				X	X							
MRC Formation				X	X							
Draft MRC ToR					X	X						
First MRC Meeting							X					
Template Development						X	X	X				
Initial Risk Tiering							X	X				
Weakness Assessment								X	X			
MRC Risk Sign-off									X	X		
Leadership Summary									X	X		
Documentation Plan										X	X	
Client Communication											X	X

Model Risk Management is a risk discipline that needs to be taken seriously, not a tax on business activity. If you get this right and the leadership team gets the memo, then ongoing activity will be as slight as it is effective. If you do not do so, the bank's model validators will keep you in the naughty seat and question everything.

Successful implementations begin with a fundamental leadership commitment:

"WE WILL UNDERSTAND OUR MODELS WELL ENOUGH TO EXPLAIN THEIR LIMITATIONS TO OUR CLIENTS."

This shifts the conversation from "what do the regulators and our clients want?" to "how do we build better products through systematic risk management?"

Before anyone else learns about model governance, your senior leadership team needs to understand what they're committing to. This isn't a one-hour briefing—it's a substantive education process covering why model failures have cost the industry billions, how governance frameworks protect business value, and what effective oversight looks like in practice.

The training covers three essential areas: recognising model risk in business decisions, understanding what effective challenge means in practice, and learning to ask the right questions during governance meetings. Leaders who complete this training understand that good model governance enhances rather than constrains business agility.

The first step is to obtain a written mandate and request the leadership team to send out a notice explaining what is happening and why it is essential, as well as emphasising that model risk is not the same as testing!

Critical artefacts:-

- Leadership training.
- Written Mandate.
- Communication to staff.

M onth One: Building the Foundation

Hurray! We are off to the races! Your first month establishes the governance infrastructure on which everything else depends. This begins with deciding what models the organisation has. Agee on a list that is meaningful and manageable, and most importantly, something that can be assigned to a model owner

The exercise is frequently eye-opening. That "simple" spreadsheet calculation turns out to influence client pricing decisions. The algorithm that segments customer communications has embedded assumptions about market behaviour. The data processing routine that seemed purely administrative contained business logic that affected outcomes.

Parallel to inventory creation, you're establishing the Model Risk Committee (MRC), the governance body that will oversee model risk across your organisation. The MRC serves as both an oversight function and an escalation pathway, ensuring that model issues reach appropriate decision-makers quickly.

The committee's Terms of Reference become your governance constitution, defining roles, responsibilities, and decision-making authority. Model owners emerge from this process with clear accountability for documenting weaknesses, monitoring performance, and escalating issues. The chairman gains the mandate to challenge development decisions and escalate concerns to senior leadership when necessary.

Critical artefacts:-

- Model list.
- Model owners agreed.
- MRC membership.

- Draft ToR for the MRC.

M onth Two: First MRC Meeting and Documentation Foundation

Month two marks a pivotal moment: the first official MRC meeting with your signed-off Terms of Reference. This is the moment your governance framework becomes operational. The committee's first act is formally agreeing on the model list and ownership.

More importantly, the MRC collectively accepts responsibility for owning the organisation's overall model risk. This shifts the conversation from individual models to portfolio-level risk management. Committee members understand they're not just reviewing technical specifications but taking accountability for ensuring the organisation understands and manages the risks inherent in its quantitative methods.

The chair will also review the model validation templates with the model owners and define the model risk tiers. A key agreement for each model owner is to quickly provide an interim overall risk tier for each model and draft details on model weaknesses, limitations of use, and the overall approach.

Critical artefacts:

- First MRC meeting minutes showing inauguration.
- The model list is formally agreed upon in the newly formed model inventory and ownership assignments.
- Agreement to adopt standard templates.

M onth Three: Proactive Client Engagement

The first activity in month three is to bilaterally agree with each model owner on their risk tier, weakness, etc., and collate for a one-off MRC to sign off on initial observations. If there are any current remediation efforts and known live issues, the MRC members review them. At this stage, the chair provides an initial summary to the leadership team.

Once the leadership team has received and understood the initial summary, the Chair and each model owner agree on the timeframe to complete the model-related documentation based on the agreed-upon templates. Since each model owner has a day job, the documentation will take several months, including a few iterations to ensure they are all at the same level.

Once the plan to build out the artefacts is agreed upon, it is time to communicate with the bank's model validation teams, outlining the MRC structure, ToR, first minutes, and project plan for documentation.

Banking validators' initial reaction is often surprise, followed by appreciation. Most vendors avoid these conversations until forced into them; however, a proactive approach signals maturity and forward-thinking that stands out in their vendor ecosystem.

Critical artefacts:

- First risk-based MRC minutes.
- Initial risk tier for each model.
- Initial weaknesses, limitations and proposed monitoring for each model.
- List of live remediation efforts.
- The project plan is to build out model validation templates.
- Communication packs for the bank's model validation teams.

The first positive response from a bank validation team creates credibility for continued investment. As joked before, tumbleweed is also a positive response.

The first three months have signalled a change in approach to model risk governance, but this is only the start. The next quarterly MRC targets completing as many model documentations as possible using the templates. If the number of models is manageable, like 8-20, then you should push to complete them within the quarter so that the model owners can peer review and sign them off at the committee.

Once completed, it is good practice to communicate with the bank validation teams, inviting them to review and provide feedback. After that, and the initial risk tiers are finalised, the focus should switch to the monitoring process and introducing the RACI-based operating model.

Banking validation teams shift from sceptical interrogation to collaborative partnership. Internal teams view governance as an enabler of innovation rather than a constraint on creativity.

The first conversation with that banking client's validation team, once a source of anxiety, becomes an opportunity to showcase capabilities that differentiate your organisation in the marketplace. The transformation from reactive compliance to competitive advantage is complete when clients begin choosing your solutions specifically because of your governance capabilities.

17

CONCLUSION

The model risk framework will continue to develop. The next phase will be to start the interoperability review, where models depend on each other. Nonetheless, it demands discipline to keep momentum so that model governance becomes instinctive rather than a chore.

Initially, I emphasised that validation is not the same as testing because that habit will stick. Only when sales teams say that strong model governance was a key factor in winning new business will people stop viewing it as just a regulatory burden.

THE MOST CRITICAL ELEMENT IS GETTING THE PROPORTIONATE PARADIGM CORRECT. TOO MUCH, TOO SOON, AND YOU WILL LOSE ORGANISATIONAL SUPPORT. TOO LITTLE, TOO SLOW, AND YOU RISK FAILING THE BANK'S MODEL VALIDATION REQUIREMENTS ENTIRELY.

Remember the cultural shifts this journey demands: openly discussing model weaknesses takes courage, but it builds trust. Allocating true model ownership goes beyond testing—it's about accountability for overall performance. As I've said throughout this book, the hardest part isn't the technical framework; it's changing how people think about models.

The regulatory demands will continue to ratchet up, so vendors who view this as merely keeping "pesky model validators at bay" are missing a competitive opportunity. Those who embrace proportionate model governance will find themselves on the list of good actors, facing fewer demands when things inevitably go wrong.

Introducing model risk governance into your organisation isn't just about compliance—it's about building better, more reliable models that serve your clients well. And that, quite simply, is a good idea.

FOR VENDORS WHO FEEL PRESSURE FROM THEIR CLIENTS' MODEL VALIDATION TEAM, MY ONLY ADVICE IS TO NOT PANIC AND EMBRACE MODEL RISK GOVERNANCE AS A PATH TO COMPETITIVE ADVANTAGE.

APPENDIX

A1

MODEL DEVELOPMENT TEMPLATE

The template below is an amalgamation of templates observed across the major banks. It has been used by vendors and tested with banking clients.

All vendors will have a variation on this template based on their specific needs and challenges, but as a first pass, this will do nicely.

The template contains minimum standards for supporting documentation for model development. The template follows industry standards around model development, so any artefacts would be acceptable to an independent validator. The use of the word "solution" in this document can easily be replaced with "code", "analysis", "model" and "methodology".

The following sections are expected to be filled in fully using concise, accurate language that an independent validator understands. This is a communication document; the gold standard is that it provides sufficient information so that a fellow practitioner can easily replicate the solution.

Executive Summary	· Single paragraph that starts with "The purpose of this solution is to ....". Examples include: Remediate known issues, improve accuracy/performance, facilitate new product deployment, reduce cost/improve efficiency/ shorten run-times · Provide the business driver and context for providing a solution · Outline the business driver for migrating to/ from home grown and vendor solutions
Model Specifics	· Model name, model inventory ID · Participants: model owner, product owner, model validator, business sponsor · Technology: platform, vendor Y/N · Model governance status, waiver status · Dates: Last delivered, documentation completed, validation completed, model risk governance committee signoff · Document history: version no, author, description, Reviewed by
Scope of Solution	· Describe the scope of the solution and how it links back to what has been agreed · Where appropriate highlight what is out of scope · Link to any client internal policies, audit assurance remediation or is part of a regulatory change program

History	· Description of previous versions of the solution, is this a replacement or enhancement
	· Summary of solution performance, limitations
	· Current interdependencies to established processes and other models
Solution Design	· Model approach including theoretical background. Compare with to those considered industry standard
	· List of assumptions and any simplifications
	· Known limitations of approach
	· Explanation of any numerical method, algorithm used and any customisation
	· Note down formulas used that are central to the solution
	· Discussion on where expert judgement or adjustments has been deployed around the data input
	· Impact of model enhancements on the current technology deployment
Solution Input Parameters	· Input parameters and source (public vs vendor vs private)
	· Approach to checking and resolving for data quality
	· Solutions such as proxying to address gaps in data
	· Itemise manual overlays and overrides

Solution Output	· Assessment of fit for purpose and stability of the model · Taxonomy of the solution outputs and how they should be used in particular if an input to decision-making or disclosure reporting · Directional relationship of each risk factor to model output, consideration of how risk factors inter-react under different conditions (Sensitivity Analysis) · Categorise each risk factor as core, non-core and not included (RNIM) · Assessment of need to improve processes from the user side (including use of spreadsheets etc)
Testing Approach	· Scope of test; functionality, methodology, calibration, benchmarking, backtesting, limited cases, convergence · Testing under general stress conditions · Input data used for testing, checks on how representative the data is of its wider application · Statistical tests when appropriate (This may include: R-squared, Error metrics, GINI Index, ROX curves, Kolmogorov-Smirnov, Hosmer-Lemeshow, etc.) · Computational performance expectations · Checks against testing bias when appropriate · Comparison of alternative approaches if applicable

Limitations and Caveats	· List where the output could be unstable or provide information that can be received incorrectly · List additional restriction or reduced performance if the solutions is implemented in a production environment · Compensating controls that need to be implemented · Plans for future developments of the model
Interaction with Model Validation	· Initial discussion with model validation, evidence the documentation has been received and understood · (potential) initial validation of the conceptual soundness of the overall model development · Evidence of initial feedback, considerations that need to either adopted or alternatively provide analysis for not adopting

Model Monitoring Approach	Examples include:
	· Minimum data quality standards, changes in external data, change in relevance, staleness, outliers
	· Performance thresholds, backtesting, statistical soundness
	· Goodness of calibration fit, benchmarking
	· New activities, volume of activity, concentration
	· Business growth/decline
	· Change in market conditions including stress
	· Publication of new generation of solutions
	· Resolution of remediation action items
Signoffs	· Author signoff
	· Reviewed-by signoff
	· Received by MRC
	· Overall Risk Tier
	· Date for follow-on review

A2

MODEL INTEROPERABILITY TEMPLATE

The template contains minimum standards for validating the interoperability between models and reflects the current Template for model validation. It is an extension of industry standards around model validation and covers how one model's output is used as an input to another.

The template describes the nature of the output of the "provider" model and the assumptions made by the "consumer" on how the (now) input is used. This provider-consumer handover model can create a "string of pearls". The purpose of this template is to describe a single link accurately during the whole process.

The following sections should be completed fully using a clear, precise language and must closely follow the provided Template for model development. This is a communication document; the ideal is that it contains enough information for a fellow practitioner to understand and replicate the validation easily during the annual cycle.

Executive Summary of the handover	· Purpose of the consumer-provider handover
	· Description of the scope and purpose of the handover
	· Overview of business imperative of the provider-consumer handover
	· Location of handover in a longer string-of-pearls
	· Model governance status, waiver status
	· Overall model risk status
	· Agreed remediation efforts

Provider-Consumer Specifics	· Model names or provider and consumer, model inventory ID · Participants: model owners, product owners, business sponsors, validation owner · Model Development documentation reference · Model Risk Assessment Level · Technology: platform, vendor Y/N · Dates: Last delivered, documentation completed, validation completed, model risk governance committee signoff · Document history: version no, author, description, Reviewed by
Scope of Handover	· Describe the scope of the handover · Describe the nature, granularity and timeliness of the data provided · Describe how the consumer uses the data, does it makes any subsequent changes in the data · Describe any underlying distributional assumption differences between the producer and consumer · Outline level of dependency the consumer has from the producer · What assumptions does the consumer make on the accuracy and availability of the information produced · Level of awareness the producer has of the appropriateness of usage

History	· Description of previous versions of the handover, is this a replacement or enhancement · Evolution of scope, assumptions, and system implementations · Evolution of optionality for a consumer to use the output from the producer, has it been imposed recently

Handover Controls and usage	· Assessment of the service agreement between the producer and consumer
	   • Production change in performance, error and issue logging
	   • Monitor of the usage by the consumer for appropriateness review by the producer
	   • Note disaggregation of risk data by the consumer

Distribution comparison	· Comparison of assumptions between producer and consumer · Comparison of granularity of (for example) time buckets · Comparability of any numerical method, algorithm used, are they compatible? · Is there evidence that a weak model is feeding data into a more sophisticated model?

Handover Parameters	· Assessment of fit for purpose and stability of the output parameters that are handed over
	· Data quality checks from consumer
	   • Catalogue use of proxying or expert judgement
	   • Additional issues when producer is a third-party vendor
	   • Additional issues when the client has a consumer model (for example for capital calculations)

Stress Testing	· Compatibility of scenario assumptions between producer and consumer
	· Review how capability to revalue assets with the context of defined macro-economic scenarios
	· How much risk information has been lost during aggregation processes
	· Check for inaccuracies by the producer get amplified by the consumer
Limitations and Caveats	· Limitations of use by the consumer
	· Monitor approach if manual overrides used
Model Risk Assessment	· Measurement and prioritisation of residual risk
	· Presentation to and feedback from both Model owners (evidence of challenge, pushback and agreed actions)
	· Impact on business decision-making – HIGH-MEDIUM-LOW
	· Assessment of handover - HIGH-MEDIUM-LOW
	· Appropriateness of model use by consumer - HIGH-MEDIUM-LOW
Signoffs	· Author signoff
	· Provider and Consumer handover signoff
	· Model risk committee signoff

A3

TEMPLATE FOR PVM

Product valuation models (PVM) produce valuation and risk measures for end-of-day books and records related to instrument and derivative positions held by an asset owner. PVM models adjust each position within a portfolio's valuation based on the most recent market data and also revalue private investments based on new information available. A PVM also calculates sensitivities such as PV01 and CR01 for all user cases and performs stress scenarios when required.

An individual PVM defines the pairing of a Product ID instance with a unique combination of the following:

- Analytical model (e.g. Black Scholes).

- Market data model (e.g. ICE direct, derived/manual, curve interpolation/extrapolation).

- Calculating engine (e.g. Murex, Internal).

Template Requirements

Each PVM requires the Model Owner to complete the following template:

Executive Summary:

- PVM ID.
- Overview of the product.
- Description of the payoff.
- Applicable markets.
- Model Owner.
- Chosen model.
- Market data model.
- Calculator system.

- Available sensitivities.
- Version history

Overall Rating

- Change in market conditions.
- Model weaknesses.
- Manual overrides.
- Limitations of use.
- Model owner risk rating.

Supporting Documentation Reference

- Model Development documentation.
- Production Testing.
- Remediation plan and status updates.
- Activity monitoring report against limitations.
- Stats on outstanding balance and volume of trades.
- The log of production issues was escalated to the model owner.
- Computational and calibration performance.

Signoffs

- Model owner signoff.
- Model risk committee sign-off.
- Date for next recertification.

A4

MRC TERMS OF REFERENCE

OK, so one to finish off is the critical terms of reference for the MRC. This is based on combining the ToR for a major bank and a major vendor. All Tors need to be validated by an audit.

MODEL RISK COMMITTEE TERMS OF REFERENCE TEMPLATE

INTRODUCTION

This template provides a practical framework for establishing the Terms of Reference for the Model Risk Committee (MRC) for vendor organisations implementing model risk governance. The MRC operates as a decision-making forum to provide sufficiently robust governance for model risk within the organisation.

The MRC's objective is to review the level of model-related risk across the entire landscape of model implementations. The MRC sets minimum standards on model documentation, design, implementation, and monitoring that enable it to respond when the level of model risk is sufficiently severe for escalation at a business leadership level.

Regarding the definition of a model, the MRC directly refers to the OCC's document SR11-7 as the primary source. Their definition is precise: "For the purposes of this document, the term model refers to a quantitative method, system, or approach that applies statistical, economic, financial, or mathematical theories, techniques, and assumptions to process input data into quantitative estimates."

A *model* consists of three components: an information input component, which delivers assumptions and data to the model; a processing component, which transforms inputs into estimates; and a reporting component, which translates the estimates into valuable business information."

The other aspect of the model definition used by the MRC is the scale. A model must have a meaningful owner and the output provide sufficiently essential business information.

The MRC defines models' scope and whether they need to be split into more granular components. The MRC applies its collective judgment to determine the appropriate level of granularity for the models in scope.

SECTION 1: PURPOSE AND MANDATE

The Leadership Team has established the Model Risk Committee to serve as a decision-making forum and offer strong governance for model risk within the organisation.

Critical Tasks:

- Provide "Second Line of Defence" oversight for model risk created using analytics and methodologies across all platforms.

- Provide oversight on key procedures within the Model Risk Framework (Development, Validation, Implementation, Monitoring) and its overall effectiveness.

- Provide the Executive Leadership Team with an overall opinion of model risk within the organisation and escalate issues deemed impactful at an enterprise level.

- Review the quality of supporting templates and documentation (including owning the Model Risk Framework document) and provide evidence of independent challenge to clients and the third line of defence.

- Act as a point of escalation for operational issues for models currently in production, planned for development, or integration.

- Ensure the completeness of the organisation's model inventory.

- Take strategic direction from the Executive Leadership Team to integrate new models into the platform, opining exclusively on the inherent model risk of new models, plus the marginal impact on overall model risk across platforms.

SECTION 2: MEMBERSHIP

Voting Members:
- **Chair**: Risk/analytics executive.
- **Members**: All appointed model owners.
- **Member**: Audit.
- **Member**: Executive Leadership Team Representative.

Meeting Attendees (as required):
- Technology representatives
- Product owners
- Subject matter experts

SECTION 3: OPERATIONAL DETAILS

- **Meeting Frequency**: Quarterly, designed to fit into the development cycle.

- **Quorum**: Chair plus three voting members in attendance.

- **Minutes**: The chair appoints a secretary to record the minutes. The chair approves the draft and circulates it to all MRC members for final approval.

- **Reporting**: The chair provides an annual (or ad hoc, on request) status update to the Executive Leadership Team on the model risk framework and MRC effectiveness.

SECTION 4: DECISION MAKING AND CHANGES

Material Changes Requiring Executive Leadership Team Approval:

- Changes to critical tasks listed in Section 1.
- Overall size of MRC.

- Meeting frequency (if less than quarterly).

Changes MRC Can Approve Internally:

- Filling vacancies within the MRC members.
- Minor procedural adjustments.
- Meeting scheduling and logistics.

Annual Review:

- The Executive Leadership Team will ratify membership in an annual cycle.
- Terms of Reference reviewed and updated as needed.

SECTION 5: KEY RESPONSIBILITIES DETAIL

Model Risk Framework Oversight:

- Review and approve model development templates and standards.
- Monitor adherence to validation requirements.
- Assess the effectiveness of model risk controls.
- Review model inventory completeness and accuracy.

Issue Management:

- Escalate significant model risk issues to the Executive Leadership Team.
- Monitor remediation of identified model deficiencies.
- Coordinate response to model-related operational incidents.

New Model Integration:

- Review proposals for new model implementations.
- Assess the impact of the model risk on the existing framework.
- Provide recommendations on model tiering and validation requirements.

Documentation and Templates:

- Own and maintain the Model Risk Framework document.
- Review and approve model development templates.
- Ensure documentation standards meet regulatory and client expectations.

SECTION 6: MEETING ADMINISTRATION

Agenda Management:

- The chair sets the agenda prior to each meeting.

- Standard agenda items include:
    - Model inventory updates
    - Validation pipeline status
    - Outstanding issues and remediation progress
    - New model proposals
    - Framework effectiveness review

Documentation:

- Meeting minutes recorded and distributed within one week
- Action items tracked and followed up
- Decisions are formally documented with rationale

Communication:

- Regular updates to the Leadership Team.
- Interface with internal audit and external validators.
- Client communication on governance standards.

A4

OVERVIEW OF BCBS 239

BCBS 239, formally known as the "Principles for effective risk data aggregation and risk reporting," represents one of the most significant regulatory frameworks governing risk management practices in modern banking. Established by the Basel Committee on Banking Supervision in January 2013, this framework emerged as a direct response to the risk management failures exposed during the 2007-2008 financial crisis. At its core, BCBS 239 mandates that systemically important banks maintain robust capabilities for aggregating risk data across their organisations and producing accurate, timely risk reports for internal decision-making and regulatory compliance.

The relevance of BCBS 239 extends far beyond traditional risk reporting into the realm of model governance and interoperability. As financial institutions increasingly rely on interconnected model ecosystems—where the output of one model serves as input to another—the principles of data traceability, transparency, and governance embedded within BCBS 239 become fundamental enablers of effective model interoperability.

BCBS 239 establishes 14 principles organised across four key areas: governance and infrastructure, risk data aggregation capabilities, risk reporting practices, and supervisory review.

- Principle 1 mandates that boards and senior management establish clear governance frameworks for risk data aggregation and reporting processes

- Principle 2 requires a robust data architecture and IT infrastructure capable of supporting accurate risk data aggregation, including integrated data taxonomies and comprehensive metadata management

- Principles 3-7: Risk Data Aggregation Capabilities. These principles establish requirements for data accuracy, completeness, timeliness, and adaptability. They mandate that institutions maintain the ability to consolidate risk data from disparate systems and business units into unified, enterprise-wide risk views.

- Principles 8-11: Risk Reporting Practices. These principles focus on producing accurate, comprehensive, clear risk reports that are distributed at appropriate frequencies to relevant stakeholders throughout the organisation.

- Principles 12-14: Supervisory Review The final principles establish the framework for supervisory assessment of compliance and mandate cooperation between institutions and regulators in addressing deficiencies.

In modern financial institutions, risk management and regulatory reporting rely heavily on interconnected model ecosystems, where models function as both producers and consumers of data. A typical "string of pearls" configuration might involve a market data model feeding price information to a valuation model, providing fair value estimates to a credit risk model, and finally feeding loss estimates into regulatory capital calculations.

BCBS 239's focus on data traceability and transparency directly tackles the governance challenges present in these Interconnected systems. The framework's requirements establish a basis for understanding and managing the complex dependencies between models, ensuring institutions can maintain effective oversight of their analytical infrastructure.

The model interoperability template referenced in contemporary risk management frameworks aligns closely with BCBS 239 principles, particularly in its emphasis on documenting and governing the handover points between model systems. Key elements of this alignment include:

-
- Transparency of Assumptions: BCBS 239's requirement for clear documentation of data transformations and business rules directly

supports the need to understand how assumptions made by provider models align with the expectations of consumer models.

- Data Quality and Integrity: The framework's emphasis on data accuracy and completeness provides the foundation for ensuring that model-to-model data transfers maintain appropriate quality standards.

- Change Management: BCBS 239's governance requirements establish processes for managing changes to data aggregation methods, which extend naturally to managing changes in model interoperability configurations.

- Risk Assessment: The framework's focus on identifying and measuring risks provides the methodology for assessing the risks associated with model interconnections and dependencies.

BCBS 239 represents more than a regulatory compliance requirement; it establishes the foundational principles for modern risk data management that enable effective model interoperability in financial institutions. The framework's emphasis on data traceability, transparency, and governance creates the infrastructure necessary for managing complex, interconnected model ecosystems while maintaining regulatory compliance and operational effectiveness.

The evolution of BCBS 239, particularly the ECB's 2024 intensification of data lineage requirements, demonstrates the increasing sophistication expected in risk data management and model governance. Institutions that embrace these requirements as opportunities to enhance their analytical capabilities, rather than merely compliance obligations, position themselves for improved risk management, operational efficiency, and competitive advantage.

As financial institutions rely more heavily on sophisticated analytical models and interconnected systems, the principles embedded within BCBS 239 will become increasingly central to effective risk management and regulatory compliance. The framework's integration with model governance practices creates a comprehensive approach to managing analytical risk that extends well beyond traditional risk reporting into the core operational capabilities of modern financial institutions.

The successful implementation of BCBS 239 in the context of model interoperability requires sustained commitment from senior management, significant technology investment, and fundamental changes in organisational approaches to data and model governance. However, institutions that make these investments effectively will be better positioned to navigate the evolving regulatory landscape while maintaining the analytical capabilities necessary for competitive success in modern financial markets.

GLOSSARY

- Artefacts Version: Controlled, hosted documents produced as a direct outcome following the governance standards and templates. These include model documentation, validation reports, monitoring results, and committee minutes that provide evidence of systematic model risk management.

- Complexity (Model): A measure of mathematical sophistication and validation difficulty. High complexity models perform complicated mathematical or statistical operations with multiple sensitive assumptions. Medium complexity models use relatively advanced operations with some embedded equations. Low complexity models perform basic analytical operations with few assumptions.

- Effective Challenge: A guiding principle for managing model risk that requires models to be subjected to independent review and validation by qualified professionals not involved in model development. The challenge function must be ongoing rather than a one-time activity, recognising that model performance can deteriorate as market conditions change.

- Escalation: The structured process for escalating model risk issues to appropriate decision-makers when problems cannot be resolved at the operational level. Clear escalation procedures define who should be involved when different types of problems occur and when model owners are required to notify senior management or clients.

- Limitations of Use: Specific ways a model might fail or produce misleading results under certain conditions. These include market conditions under which the model becomes unreliable, data requirements that might not always be met, assumptions that become problematic during stress periods, and computational constraints affecting performance.

- Materiality (Model): A measure of potential business impact if the model produces incorrect results. High materiality models are essential for firm performance or client capital calculations. Medium materiality models cover moderate risk factors with manageable consequences. Low materiality models have limited impact on critical business decisions.

- Model: A quantitative method, system, or approach that applies statistical, economic, financial, or mathematical theories, techniques, and assumptions to process input data into quantitative estimates. Consists of three components: information input, processing algorithm, and reporting output that translates estimates into valuable business information.

- Model Inventory: The central repository that maintains comprehensive records of all models throughout their lifecycle, serving as the authoritative source for model governance information. Captures essential metadata including model identification, purpose, technical specifications, ownership details, and current governance status.

- Model Owner: The designated individual accountable for a model's performance and appropriate use. Ownership extends beyond technical oversight, including business responsibility for decisions informed by model outputs. Model owners must understand model weaknesses, monitor performance, and escalate issues appropriately.

- Model Risk is the potential for adverse consequences arising from decisions based on incorrect or misused model outputs. This can lead to financial loss, poor business and strategic decision-making, or damage to reputation. Model risk increases when models are used inappropriately or when multiple models interact unexpectedly.

- Model Risk Committee (MRC): A risk-based governance function that reviews artefacts provided by the model risk governance process, assesses whether overall model risk is appropriate for the enterprise, and escalates to leadership when it is not. It is not a talking shop or validator but a decision-making body with clear accountability.

- Model Risk Lifecycle: The structured framework for managing quantitative models from initial conception through decommissioning. Six interconnected stages: defining business case, developing model, validation, production implementation, performance monitoring, and risk management, supported by a central model inventory.

- Model Risk Management: An enterprise-level framework for identifying, assessing, and controlling model-related risks across the organisation. Encompasses validation as one component within a broader approach that considers strategic risks, model concentration, and cumulative effects of model deployment.

- Model Validation: A set of analytical activities designed to assess whether individual models work as intended. Validators challenge model design choices, test mathematical implementations and evaluate performance against stated objectives. Operates at the model level, focusing on technical adequacy.

- Monitoring: The ongoing oversight activities that ensure models continue to operate effectively throughout their operational lifecycle. Includes performance monitoring, stability monitoring, usage monitoring, threshold monitoring, comparison monitoring, and operational monitoring to detect model degradation and data quality issues.

- Operational Risk: In the model context, the risk arises from inadequate or failed internal processes, people, and systems affecting model performance. Includes failed production jobs, manual override frequency, system failures, and operational indicators that suggest models are encountering conditions they weren't designed to handle.

- Override (Manual): Human intervention in model processes where users adjust or override model outputs when they believe results are inappropriate for specific circumstances. Requires clear policies about when overrides are appropriate, approval processes for significant adjustments, and comprehensive documentation of rationale and frequency.

- Proportionality: The principle that recognises not all models pose equal risk, requiring different oversight levels based on materiality and complexity. Prevents over-engineering governance for simple models while ensuring adequate oversight for complex, high-risk models. Essential for efficient resource allocation and effective risk management.

- RACI Framework: An operating model that defines roles for model operations: Responsible (Operations Lead for smooth running), Accountable (Model Owner for overall outcomes), Consulted (Other Model Owners on issues), and Informed (Leadership Team and stakeholders on material matters). Provides clarity during model failures or unusual conditions.

- Remediation: The systematic process of addressing identified model deficiencies or performance issues. Includes developing corrective action plans, implementing compensating controls, monitoring progress, and reporting to governance committees. May involve model modifications, enhanced monitoring, or usage restrictions.

- Ronseal Test: The fundamental question, "Does the model do what it says on the tin?" addresses model integrity. It asks whether the model implementation aligns with its theoretical design and intended purpose. The test is named after the paint company's advertising slogan, emphasising straightforward functionality.

- SR 11-7 "Guidance on Model Risk Management": A document issued jointly by the Federal Reserve and the Office of the Comptroller of the Currency in April 2011. Established comprehensive principles for model risk management following the 2008 financial crisis, emphasising effective challenge, model ownership, and systematic risk management frameworks.

- String of Pearls: The risk arising from model chains where the output of one model becomes the input to another model. Can amplify model risks in ways that aren't immediately obvious, requiring special attention to ensure overall system reliability and compatibility of underlying assumptions.

- Testing: The process of checking that code executes correctly according to specifications and operates efficiently in production environments. Different from validation, testing focuses on technical functionality rather than challenging model choices or assessing appropriateness for intended use.

- Tier Classification: A four-tier structure combining materiality and complexity assessments to determine appropriate governance levels. Tier 1 (maximum oversight) for high materiality/complexity models; Tier 2 (substantial oversight); Tier 3 (moderate oversight); Tier 4 (minimal oversight) for low-risk models with basic governance requirements.

- Tumbleweed: A colloquial term for the best outcome in model governance interactions - when validators have no questions or concerns, indicating effective governance has addressed potential issues proactively. Represents a smooth passage through validation processes without significant challenges or delays.

- Validation: Independent assessment by qualified practitioners to evaluate whether developed models meet their intended purpose and operate within acceptable risk parameters. This includes documentation review, data validation, methodology review, and evidence challenge to provide an essential independent challenge for model choices and implementation.

- Weaknesses (Model): Acknowledged limitations or vulnerabilities in model design, implementation, or application that could affect reliability or accuracy. Honest assessment of where models might fail or produce misleading results, requiring transparent documentation to build validator confidence and enable appropriate risk management.